GENDER AND FAMILY

Edited by Viviene E. Cree

First published in Great Britain in 2015 by

Policy Press
University of Bristol
1-9 Old Park Hill
Bristol
BS2 8BB
UK
t: +44 (0)117 954 5940
pp-info@bristol.ac.uk
www.policypress.co.uk

North America office:
Policy Press
c/o The University of Chicago Press
1427 East 60th Street
Chicago, IL 60637, USA
t: +1 773 702 7700
f: +1 773-702-9756
sales@press.uchicago.edu
www.press.uchicago.edu

© Policy Press 2015

ISBN 978-1-4473-2191-0 Paperback
ISBN 978-1-4473-2192-7 ePub
ISBN 978-1-4473-2193-4 Kindle

British Library Cataloguing in Publication Data
A catalogue record for this book is available from the British Library.

Library of Congress Cataloging-in-Publication Data
A catalog record for this book has been requested.

Cover design by Policy Press
Printed in Great Britain by www.4edge.co.uk

ALSO AVAILABLE IN THIS SERIES

Contents

Contributors

Liz Beddoe is an Associate Professor in the School of Counselling, Human Services and Social Work at the University of Auckland in New Zealand. Publications include *Social work practice for promoting health and well-being: Critical issues* (2014), edited with Jane Maidment.

Sally Brown is a medical sociologist at the School of Medicine, Pharmacy and Health, Durham University. She is interested in qualitative health research methods as well as teenage well-being, men's health, and the sociology of screening, diagnosis and risk. A recent paper is: 'They think it's all up to the girls: gender, risk and responsibility for contraception', *Culture, Health and Sexuality*, published online: 1 October 2014.

Gary Clapton is a Senior Lecturer in Social Work at the University of Edinburgh. He specialises in adoption and fostering, child welfare and protection and fathers. His work includes *Social work with fathers: Positive practice* (2013) and a number of papers directed to changing current policies and practices in Scotland.

Viviene E. Cree is Professor of Social Work Studies at the University of Edinburgh. She is a qualified youth and community and social worker. She has carried out extensive research into social work history, the profession and children's services and has published widely. A recent book is *Becoming a social worker: Global narratives* (2013).

Dawn Mannay is a Lecturer in Social Science (Psychology) at Cardiff University. Her research interests revolve around class, education, gender, generation, national identity, violence and inequality. A recent paper is 'Who should do the dishes now? Exploring gender and housework in contemporary urban South Wales', in *Contemporary Wales*, vol 27, no 1, pp 21–39.

Maggie Mellon, MSc, CQSW and Dip Child Protection, is a registered social worker with many years' experience, now working as an independent consultant. She writes regularly on social work issues for national and professional media and is currently Vice Chair of the British Association of Social Workers.

Mark Smith is a Senior Lecturer and current Head of Social Work at the University of Edinburgh. He has an interest in abuse allegations made against care staff and is currently working on an ESRC-funded project centred on allegations against the former BBC disc jockey, Jimmy Savile. One of his recent books is *Residential child care in practice: Making a difference* (2013), written with Leon Fulcher and Peter Doran.

Morena Tartari is a Lecturer in Sociology at the University of Padua, Italy. Her research interests include media, moral panic and regulation, deviance and social problems. Her latest publication is 'Moral panic and paedophilia: where's the risk?', in *Moral panics in the contemporary world* (2013), edited by Julian Petley, Charles Critcher and Jason Hughes.

Stuart Waiton is Senior Lecturer in Sociology and Criminology at Abertay University and author of *Scared of the kids: Curfews, crime and the regulation of young people* (2008) and *The politics of antisocial behaviour: Amoral panics* (2007). His latest book is entitled *Snobs law: Criminalising football fans in an age of intolerance* (2012).

Series editors' preface

Viviene E. Cree, Gary Clapton and Mark Smith

This book series begins and ends with a question: how useful are ideas of moral panic to the social issues and anxieties that confront us today? Forty years on from the publication of Stan Cohen's seminal study *Folk Devils and Moral Panics*, does this remain a helpful way of thinking about social concerns, or should the concept be consigned to the sociological history books as an amusing, but ultimately flawed, theoretical device? 'Moral panic' is, after all, one of the foremost sociological terms that has crossed over from academic to public discourse; in doing so, it has lost a great deal of its rigour and, arguably, its value. All the contributors to the series are, in their own ways, engaging critically with the relevance of moral panic ideas for their own understandings of some of the most pressing personal, professional and political concerns of the day. They do not all come up with the same conclusions, but they do agree that moral panics – no matter how we think of them – focus on the social issues that worry us most.

The book series takes forward findings from an Economic and Social Research Council (ESRC) sponsored research seminar series that ran between 2012 and 2014 at events across the UK. The seminar series was designed to mark the 40th anniversary of *Folk Devils and Moral Panics*; and to bring together international and UK academics, researchers and practitioners from a range of disciplines to debate and discuss moral panics in the 21st century. The three main organisers had, independently of one another, written about events and happenings that had caused great anxiety within social work and within society as a whole: satanic abuse (Clapton, 1993); sex trafficking (Cree, 2008); abuse in residential childcare (Smith, 2008 and 2010). In each case, we had challenged accepted accounts of the issues and asked questions about the real-life (often negative) consequences of holding particular conceptualisations of these difficult topics. We had not, at that time, used the concept of moral panic as the foremost tool for analysis, but we had all been interested in the ideas of discourse, labelling, deviancy amplification and social control, all of which connect with ideas of moral panic. With the 40th anniversary imminent, we saw this as offering an opportunity to revisit this, asking: what relevance does the idea of moral panic have for an examination of 21st-century social issues and anxieties?

The seminar series produced a number of outcomes: articles, blogs and the collection of papers included in these bytes. However, the collection is broader than the seminar series in two key ways: firstly, some chapters were especially commissioned because it was felt that there was a gap in the collection or because the writer had a particularly interesting approach to the issues; secondly, each of the books in this series ends with an afterword written by a social work practitioner who has been invited to reflect on the contributions from the perspective of practice. This demonstrates not only our commitment to knowledge exchange more generally, but also our belief that moral panic ideas have special relevance for social work.

Moral panics and social work

Although 'moral panic' is a sociological idea that has widespread intellectual interest, it has, as Cohen (1998) acknowledges, special relevance for social work. Social work as an academic discipline and a profession plays a central role in the process of defining social issues and then trying to do something about them – that is our job! So we have to be particularly alert to the part we play within this. We are, in moral panic parlance, 'moral entrepreneurs' and 'claims makers': we tell society (government, policy makers, other practitioners, members of the public) what the social problems are, how they should be understood and how they should be addressed. We do so, in 21st-century terms, through secular, professional and academic discourse, but at heart, what we are expressing is a set of ideas about how we should live and what it is to be human. In other words, we remain a 'moral' and, at times, moralising profession.

The concept of moral panic reminds us that our deeply held attitudes and values have origins and consequences in the real world, both positive and negative. And sometimes they are not the origins or consequences we expect them to be. Hence the lens of moral panic highlights the ways in which social issues that begin with real concerns may lead to the labelling and stigmatising of certain behaviours and individuals; they may precipitate harsh and disproportionate legislation; they may make people more fearful and society a less safe place. Focusing on some social issues may distract attention away from other, underlying concerns; so a focus on trafficking may, for example, ignore the realities of repressive, racist immigration policies, just as a focus on internet pornography may lead to legislation that undermines individual freedom, and a focus on child protection may inhibit our capacity to support families, as Featherstone et al (2014) have identified. These are not issues about which we, as editors and contributors to this series, have answers – but we do have questions. And it is our firm belief that social work must engage with these questions if we are to practise in ways that are truly emancipatory and in line with the social work profession's social justice principles.

A particular moment in the history of moral panics?

The years 2013 and 2014 have proved to be a very particular time in the history of moral panics for two, very different, reasons. The first reason is that a number of key protagonists from the early theoretical writing on deviance, moral panics and the state died in 2013 and early 2014.

- Stan Cohen, sociologist and author of *Folk Devils and Moral Panics* (1972), *Visions of Social Control* (1985), *States of Denial* (2001) and numerous other publications, died in January 2013.
- Geoffrey Pearson, social work professor and author of *The Deviant Imagination* (1975) and *Hooligan: A History of Respectable Fears* (1983), died in April 2013.

- Jock Young, criminologist and author of *The Drugtakers* (1971) and many other studies including, most recently, *The Criminological Imagination* (2011), died in November 2013.
- Stuart Hall, critical theorist, founding editor of *New Left Review* and author with Charles Critcher and others of *Policing the Crisis* (1978), died in February 2014.

We wished to mark the contribution of these great thinkers, and so we have included a commentary on one of them within each byte in the series. This is not to suggest that they are the only people who have written about contemporary social issues in this way; in fact, Geoffrey Pearson was more concerned with the persistent nature of what he called 'respectable discontents' than about the sporadic eruptions of moral panics. But, as the series will demonstrate, theorists from a wide range of academic disciplines have continued to engage with the concept of moral panics over the 40-plus years since 1972, sometimes arguing for its continuing value (for example, Goode and Ben-Yehuda, 1994) and at other times favouring alternative explanations, such as those around risk (for example, Beck, 1992, 1999) and moral regulation (for example, Hunt, 1999). More recently, scholars have attempted to move 'beyond the heuristic', to develop a way of thinking about moral panic that both informs, and continues 'to be informed by, movements and developments in social theory' (Rohloff and Wright, 2010, p 419).

The second reason why this has been a special time is because of what has been called the 'Jimmy Savile effect' in numerous press and media reports. It is difficult to discuss the scandal around Jimmy Savile, TV presenter and prolific sex offender, who died in October 2011, in a dispassionate way. In September and October 2012, almost a year after his death, claims emerged that Savile had committed sexual abuse over many years, with his victims ranging from girls and boys to adults. By October 2012, allegations had been made to 13 British police forces, and a series of inquiries followed. The revelations around the Jimmy Savile affair encouraged others to come forward and claim that they had been abused by celebrities: Stuart Hall (TV presenter, not critical theorist), Rolf Harris, Max Clifford and many others have been investigated and prosecuted. These events have encouraged us to ask wider questions in articles and blogs about physical and sexual abuse, and about potentially negative fall-out from the furore around historic abuse. This has not been easy: how do we get across the reality that we are not minimising the damage that abuse can cause, while at the same time calling for a more questioning approach to victimisation and social control? These questions remain challenging as we move forward.

The series

This series of bytes introduces a collection of papers that engage with a social issue through the lens of moral panic. It will be evident from the chapters that, as editors, we have not imposed a 'moral panic straightjacket' on the contributors; nor do we hold to the notion that there is one 'Moral Panic Theory' with a capital T. Instead, contributors have been invited to consider moral panic ideas very broadly, focusing on their capacity to add to a deeper understanding of the social problem under discussion. Because of this, the series offers a number of opportunities for those who are already familiar with the concept of moral panic and for those who are not. For those who have been thinking about moral panic ideas for years, the series will serve as a new 'take' on some of the puzzling aspects of moral panic theories. For those who are coming across the notion of moral panic for the first time, or have only everyday knowledge of it, the case-study examples of particular social issues and anxieties contained in each chapter will serve as an introduction not only to moral panic as a theoretical concept, but also to what, we hope, might become a new avenue of critical inquiry for readers in the future.

The series is divided into four short volumes ('bytes'): *Gender and family*; *Childhood and youth*; *The state*; and *Moral regulation*. Each byte contains an introduction, which includes a short retrospective on one of the four early theorists whom we have already identified. Five chapters follow, each exploring the case study of one social issue, asking how useful a moral panic lens is (or is not) to understanding this social problem. Each byte ends with an afterword written by a social work practitioner. The four bytes are also available as a single volume – *Revisiting moral panics*, featuring an introduction to Moral Panic Theory by Charles Critcher – with the aim of reaching as wide an audience as possible.

The books in this series should be read as an opening conversation. We are not seeking either consensus or closure in publishing this series; quite the opposite, our aim is to ask questions – of social problems, of professional practice and of ourselves. In doing so, we pay homage to Cohen's (1998, p 112) challenge to 'stay unfinished'; instead of seeking to resolve the contradictions and complexities that plague theory and practice, we must, he argues, be able to live with ambiguity. The series may help us and others to do just that, and, in doing so, may contribute towards the building of a more tolerant, open social work practice and a more tolerant, open society.

Acknowledgement

With thanks to the ESRC for funding the seminar series 'Revisiting Moral Panics: A Critical Examination of 21st Century Social Issues and Anxieties' (ES/J021725/1) between October 2012 and October 2014.

References

Beck, U. (1992) *Risk society: Towards a new modernity*, London: Sage.

Beck, U. (1999) *World risk society*, Cambridge: Polity Press.

Clapton, G. (1993) *Satanic abuse controversy: Social workers and the social work press*, London: University of North London Press.

Cohen, S. (1972) *Folk devils and moral panics: The creation of the mods and rockers*, London: MacGibbon and Kee Ltd.

Cohen, S. (1985) *Visions of social control: Crime, punishment and classification*, Cambridge: Polity Press.

Cohen, S. (1998) *Against criminology*, London: Transaction Publishers.

Cohen, S. (2001) *States of denial knowing about atrocities and suffering*, Cambridge: Polity Press.

Cree, V.E. (2008) 'Confronting sex-trafficking: lessons from history', *International Social Work*, vol 51, no 6, pp 763–76.

Featherstone, B., White, S. and Morris, K. (2014) *Re-imagining child protection: Towards humane social work with families*, Bristol: Policy Press.

Goode, E. and Ben-Yehuda, N. (1994) *Moral panics: The Social construction of deviance*, Oxford: Blackwell.

Hall, S., Critcher, C., Jefferson, T., Clarke, J. and Roberts, B. (1978) *Policing the crisis: Mugging, the state and law and order*, London: Macmillan.

Hunt, A. (1999) *Governing morals: A social history of moral regulation*, Cambridge University Press, New York.

Pearson, G. (1975) *The deviant imagination: Psychiatry, social work and social change*, London: Macmillan.

Pearson, G. (1983) *Hooligan: A history of respectable fears,* London: Macmillan.

Rohloff, A. and Wright, S. (2010) 'Moral panic and social theory: beyond the heuristic', *Current Sociology*, vol 58, no 3, pp 403–19.

Smith, M. (2008) 'Historical abuse in residential child care: an alternative view', *Practice: Social Work in Action*, vol 20, no 1, pp 29–41.

Smith, M. (2010) 'Victim Narratives of historical abuse in residential child care: do we really know what we think we know?', *Qualitative Social Work*, vol 9, no 3, pp 303–20.

Young, J. (1971) *The drugtakers: The social meaning of drug use*, London: Paladin.

Young, J. (2011) *The criminological imagination*, Cambridge: Polity Press.

Introduction

Viviene E. Cree

To open each of the bytes in this series, we introduce the work of a key theorist within the 'moral panic' genre. The work of Stanley Cohen has played a central part in the creation of ideas around moral panic and these, as will be shown, have developed over time. Many of Cohen's ideas are reflected in the chapters in this volume and throughout the series, while others have been taken forward in other writing in the field.

Stanley Cohen

Stanley Cohen (Stan) was born on 23 February 1942 in Johannesburg, South Africa and studied Sociology and Social Work at the University of Witwatersrand. He moved to the UK in 1963 with his wife, Ruth, where he worked as a psychiatric social worker and PhD student at the London School of Economics (LSE), studying social reactions to vandalism. Cohen was appointed to his first academic position in 1967, at the University of Durham, and in 1968, with Jock Young and others, he set up the first National Deviancy Conference, an initiative that was to challenge conventional ideas about crime and criminology for years to come. He moved to Essex University in 1972, where he became a professor in 1974. Stan and Ruth relocated to Israel in 1980; Stan was professor at the Hebrew University of Jerusalem until 1994. He returned to the LSE in 1995, where, as Chair in Sociology, he helped to establish the Centre for the Study of Human Rights.

Stan Cohen is widely held to be one of the world's pre-eminent sociologists; that he began his career as a social worker makes absolute sense, given his lifelong concern for theory developed from practice, for making connections between the personal and the political, and his deep concern for human rights. Cohen's first book, *Folk Devils and Moral Panics* (1972) was the book of his PhD study on the 1960s battles between mods and rockers. Here Cohen argued that the social reaction to the minor skirmishes between young people on the beaches in Clacton accelerated their bad behaviour and led to a widespread moral panic centred on young people. This book marked the beginning of the translation of the idea of moral panics from academic to everyday usage and, unsurprisingly, to a great deal of misuse of the concept too, as Cohen was acutely aware. He went on to write *Psychological Survival* (1972), with the sociologist Laurie Taylor, exploring the closed emotional world within the maximum security H-wing at Durham Prison. *Prison Secrets* (1976) followed. In this, he again focused on prison, this time introducing the idea of 'dispersal of control' to describe the ways in which the state ever extends its reach into everyday life. *Visions of Social Control* (1985) took this idea further, pointing out that even seemingly benign interventions in the name of 'community' can be subverted and become ever-stricter measures of social control. In 1988, he published a collection of essays entitled *Against Criminology*, in which he promoted a 'sceptical' sociology of crime, deviance and control, in opposition to the statistically oriented correctionalism that pervaded criminology at the time.

Cohen's last book, *States of Denial, Knowing about Atrocities and Suffering* (2001), is an astonishing book that brings together his personal experience (in South Africa and later in Israel) with his criminological knowledge and insights and his passionate belief in human rights. He begins the book in South Africa, in his childhood home. Here he asks: how was it that he, as a young child, knew and didn't know about the injustice experienced by the indigenous black people? He goes on to ask: how do we see and not see atrocities and suffering throughout the world? His call in the end is that we must not be bystanders – we must act. This is a powerful message for social work, a profession that is so thoroughly implicated in social control and yet one that has such potential to make a difference in the lives of those who are disadvantaged. It is also a powerful message for all humankind – that we each have responsibility to challenge oppression where we see it.

In a small way, this book series attempts to live up to the challenge set by Cohen. Each of the chapters that follows in this byte engages critically with something that has been identified as a social problem, and tries to encourage new ways of thinking about it. Stan Cohen, in the last months of his life, was very interested in and supportive of our moral panic project. We can only hope that he would have welcomed the outcome.

Stanley Cohen died on 7 January 2013.

Content of this byte

The chapters in this byte all begin from the starting-point of an exploration of gender and the family, asking if and how the concept of moral panic has meaning for the ways in which we think about, and act towards, gender and the family today. This book, along with others in the series, is an eclectic collection; people are writing from different disciplinary backgrounds and different countries, and they have different 'takes' on moral panic theory. We have not tried to reconcile these differences; instead, readers are invited to make up their own minds or, rather, to ask their own questions in response to the questions posed by the authors. Not only are the chapters in this book a varied collection, but the book itself is, in important ways, incomplete – it cannot pretend, in so few chapters, to say everything that might be said about gender and the family today. There is, for example, no chapter about either men or fathers; this absence is one that we intend to address as our work progresses in the future. In spite of these cautionary words, this byte offers an exciting, and at times provocative, group of chapters that explore the connections between ideas of gender, class, 'race', youth and 'the family', and highlights the importance of not taking things for granted and of questioning the very basis of our beliefs. The social issues identified here all have consequences, often negative ones, for individuals and for society; such is the power of power panics.

Chapter One, by Morena Tartari, tackles head on two social problems that have emerged in Italy in recent years (and, of course, are familiar throughout the world): child abuse and intimate-partner violence, or rather, 'femicide'. In her chapter, Tartari argues that while these are legitimate subjects of concern, the social and political reaction to them has been disproportionate, leading to the passing of extremely harsh legislation against those deemed to be 'perpetrators' such as 'paedophiles'. What concerns her more, however, is the impact that these moral panics and the resultant increased anxiety have had on women and children. She asserts that women and children have increasingly been presented as weak and in need of protection, allowing the state to intervene in ever-stronger ways.

The next three chapters explore the intersections between ideas of femininity, motherhood, social class and 'race' in three very different contexts: South Wales (Dawn Mannay, Chapter Two), New Zealand (Liz Beddoe, Chapter Three) and the North of England (Sally Brown, Chapter Four). Dawn Mannay's chapter explores 'respectable and acceptable femininities' as they are negotiated in a discourse of what she describes as a 'pervasive discourse of lack, stigma and classed moral panics'. Her chapter builds from her own study of mothers and daughters in one of the most deprived communities in South Wales, one that, she argues, is illustrative of a 'spatial folk devil' that stigmatises all who grow up there. Nevertheless, strategies of resistance are evident in the women's lives, as demonstrated in the stories of Melanie and her daughter, Adele.

Liz Beddoe's Chapter Three reflects similar themes, but this time examines them in the context of the media characterisation of 'feral families' in the UK and New Zealand. She begins with an account of the characterisation of poor families in the UK, seen in TV programmes such as *Benefits Street*, and government initiatives such as the Troubled Families Programme (Chapters Two and Four of The state (byte 3 in this series). From here, she opens up the subject to consider the connections being made in this discourse of moral panic between poverty, welfare dependency, child abuse, family violence and Maori families in New Zealand. She argues that this moral panic is not accidental; it is, rather, part of a deliberate tactic to target the 'underclass'.

In Chapter Four Sally Brown brings us back to the UK, this time to teenage parenting in the North of England. Here she examines the reality that while teenage pregnancy and motherhood figures have fallen in the UK, so concern for teenage pregnancy and motherhood has grown. The underlying assumption, she argues, is that the 'wrong kind' of women are becoming pregnant and having babies; teenage mothers are presented as 'bad' mothers who lack the necessary experience and parenting skills. Sally's research disputes this, and she concludes that the panic about teenage pregnancy and parenting is closely aligned to the panic about welfare 'scroungers' and the need to reduce the role of the welfare state.

The byte ends with a provocative contribution from Stuart Waiton, already a well-known figure in the body of literature on moral panics. He begins with the suggestion that as moral discourses in society have declined, so the panic about the family that we are currently experiencing in the UK might best be described as an 'amoral panic'. He then picks up the idea of 'early intervention', much loved in social work and social policy circles, and argues that by increasingly intervening early, the state extends its role and its power in ways that we have not begun to imagine. While the focus might, in theory, seem to be on families in poverty, the panic about parenting is generalised or normalised – we all become targets of intervention, and the autonomous self is diminished. This is a challenging place to end this first byte, and the idea is picked up in subsequent bytes.

References

Cohen, S. (1972) *Folk devils and moral panics: The creation of the mods and rockers*, London: MacGibbon and Kee Ltd.

Cohen, S. (1985) *Visions of social control: Crime, punishment and classification*, Cambridge: Polity Press.

Cohen, S. (1988) *Against criminology*, London: Transaction Publishers.

Cohen, S. (2001) *States of denial: Knowing about atrocities and suffering*, Cambridge: Polity Press.

Cohen, S. and Taylor, L. (1972) *Psychological survival: Experience of long-term imprisonment*, London: Pelican Books Ltd.

Cohen, S. and Taylor, L. (1976) *Prison secrets*, London: Pluto Press.

ONE

Women and children first: contemporary Italian moral panics and the role of the state

Morena Tartari

Introduction

This chapter interrogates moral panic through examination of the treatment of child abuse and femicide in Italy in recent years. The discussion builds on my own research in this field. I will argue that child abuse and intimate partner violence are social problems that have both generated moral panics in contemporary Italy. These issues are real phenomena and they must not be neglected or denied, but their severity may have been over-emphasised and over-represented within the public and media arenas, giving rise to peaks of public concern and anxiety that, in turn, have provoked reactions that can be seen as moral panics. As we will see, waves of concern about child abuse were apparent in the years 2006 to 2009; then a new kind of phenomenon emerged in 2012: 'femicide'. This term and its menace spread through different arenas under the pressure of feminist movements, moral entrepreneurs and politicians, thus provoking widespread social alarm and calls for action.

The chapter discusses my research into the emergence of these concerns and panics, the role of moral entrepreneurs and the disproportionality of the reaction, as well as the consequent legislation and the role of the state in reinforcing the social concerns. In what follows, I first explain how we can understand these issues as moral panics and what makes them such; then I identify some of the key ingredients of these contemporary moral panics; lastly, I discuss how the state can be seen as a particular kind of definer with strong power and control over the legitimisation of social concerns. I begin, however, with a brief introduction to the methodological approach taken in my study.

The approach used in my study

The methodological approach of this study is based on a flexible form of grounded theory (Charmaz, 2006) and the use of sensitising concepts (Blumer, 1969), stemming from the seminal work of Cohen (1972), Hall et al (1978), Beck (1992), Jenkins (1992), Goode and Ben-Yehuda (1994), Beck and Beck-Gernsheim (1995), Critcher (2003 and 2009) and Hier (2011). The corpus of data is constituted by national newspaper articles (from 1992 to 2013), TV programmes (2007 for the child abuse moral panic and 2012–13 for the femicide moral panic), 60 in-depth interviews with social actors involved in the emergence of panics, ethnographies of conferences and public events about child abuse and femicide, and journalism essays about these issues.

Child abuse and femicide as moral panics

Waves of heightened public concern about children and child abuse emerged between the 1980s and the 1990s across the United States and Europe, leading to numerous judicial inquiries (as discussed in full by de Young, 2004 and Jenkins, 1998). In particular, the focus of concern was a new kind of sex crime, the ritual abuse of children; and the perpetrators (the 'folk devils' in moral panic language) were held to be day-care providers and others who had contact with the children at the day-care centres. Although a great many of those who were accused of sexual abuse at this time were later acquitted, there were calls for changes in the law, sometimes successful. The moral entrepreneurs who had played such a significant role in the UK and the US panics also became well known in Europe, where they disseminated their studies at staff training events for professionals. Furedi (2004) has described this as a vital element in enhancing what he has identified as 'therapy culture', in other words vulnerability has become a salient feature of people, and the therapeutic culture fuels a representation of people as powerless and ill. Hence the problems of everyday life must be read as emotional problems, and this exacerbates audiences' anxieties concerning 'risks' and 'emotional damage'. In Italy, some professionals organised themselves into associations that became pressure groups and interest groups, and entered media arenas. They led moral crusades, sensitising parents to the innumerable risks for children and the danger of emotional damage, thus producing anxieties for both parents and a wider public. In particular, therapy culture gained consensus in social services and among social workers, and this engendered child-abuse moral panics.

Concerns about femicide are more recent; the term first appeared in Italy in 2012. Previously, Lagarde, a Mexican academic anthropologist and politician, had coined the term to describe the social phenomenon of the women killed in her country. She campaigned for the Mexican government to acknowledge the crime of femicide by extending the meaning of the term to encompass all crimes of hate and violence against women. The pioneering work of the feminist criminologists Russell and Radford (1992) identified femicide as a criminological category and brought it to public attention. In the Italian media, the term was used in a broad sense to refer to different situations ranging from abuse to murder. The femicide moral panic, which began as a cultural operation of sensitisation, followed the protests of the left-wing and feminist movements against the sexual scandals of Prime Minister Berlusconi. Campaigners railed against the image of the 'woman as sexual object' that had been highlighted by these scandals and by the media that Berlusconi owned; they also bemoaned the general degeneration of behaviour, and the potential threat of Berlusconi's re-election. In the wake of the political controversy, the media concentrated its attention on this kind of crime.

It is my contention that campaigns centred on child abuse and femicide have all the fundamental ingredients of a moral panic; the process of their development and decline is similar to the processes described by the classic moral panic models, as will now be explored in more detail.

Key aspects of the child abuse and femicide moral panics in contemporary Italy

Analysis of national newspaper articles between 1992 and 2013 clearly demonstrates the course taken by the panic around child abuse in Italy, as seen in the disproportionality between real crime rates, on the one hand, and concerns and reactions in the media and public arenas on the other (Tartari, 2013 and 2014). The terms 'paedophilia' and 'child abuse' entered the media lexicon in the 1980s, but it was in the 1990s that their frequencies increased exponentially, with a similar trend for each of them. The term 'paedophilia' now predominates, while the term 'child abuse' has become less visible. 'The paedophile' has become unequivocally a 'folk devil'; his representation is influenced by the construction of childhood in Western societies (Zelizer, 1994; James, Jenks and Prout, 1998), where the risks and menaces towards all children are perceived to have increased (Beck and Beck-Gernsheim, 1995).

The two main Italian national newspapers give different coverage to the perceived problem of child abuse: the left-wing newspaper emphasises social issues like this to a much greater extent. The media reflect the increase of public concern, and expert opinions enter the public debate. Interest groups are effective in gaining consensus among the elites, and moral entrepreneurs are efficient in drawing public attention to paedophilia issues – making a strong contribution to the creation of local moral panics. The emotional and moral components are over-represented in the discourses of moral entrepreneurs, and their claims are taken up by the state and its key institutions.

Politicians have progressively involved themselves in the child-abuse moral panics. The discourses of right-wing politicians stress the value of the traditional and patriarchal family, shifting the attention to paedophilia in order to underline the extra-familial nature of child abuse. In parallel, they promote a policy of uncertainty based on the sensationalisation of crimes and insecurity (Maneri, 2013). Left-wing politicians meanwhile focus their attention on children as victims to be protected, as subjects 'at risk of suffering by the hands of adults' (Critcher, 2009). This clashes with a progressive representation of children as participative subjects with agency: autonomous and active.

The child-abuse moral panics in Italy produced changes in the law, with the introduction of harsher penalties for crimes related to child abuse. The state funded public and private centres for the prevention and treatment of child abuse; it promoted campaigns against paedophilia; it supported public events against the phenomenon; and, through ministers, it sometimes took direct action by issuing ad hoc decrees. The state was receptive to the child-abuse moral panic and legitimated the claims raised by interest groups. The media, interest groups, experts and moral entrepreneurs, and the state with its institutions, created spirals of signification that led to moral panic.

Analysis of newspaper articles shows that the problem of femicide is also over-represented in the press, specifically in one of the main national newspapers that supports the social protests of left-wing women. While in 2006 cases of violence against women in the crime news were predominantly presented as murders of women by immigrants (Giomi and Tonello, 2013), by 2012 the focus was on intimate-partner violence. The victims were women involved in intimate relationships, not 'women in general'; the offenders were their partners, husbands, ex-partners or ex-husbands – men with whom they had had a relationship. The folk devil, in this instance, was now the 'man as a man'. Headlines like 'We have become the country where the male has a licence to kill' became common. Crimes figures were either over-emphasised or ignored or misused (see, for example, data from ISTAT and EUROSTAT). The publishing industry became interested in the phenomenon, and during 2012–13 the number of critical essays and popular works on femicide rapidly increased.

It is important to note that the interest groups involved in this moral panic were politically close to the interest groups of the child-abuse panic. The feminist movement and its related associations sought to raise funds from government sources, the aim being to reactivate already-existing centres for the protection of women or to create new centres for the treatment of women 'at risk' of violence, or victims of it. The sensitisation concerned risks and dangers that might originate from male power, from male cultural dominance and from the imbalanced relationships between men and women. The woman was represented as a victim, weak, unable to protect herself, in need of emotional, psychological, social and financial support. Left-wing politicians were active in underlining the 'gender question', while right-wing politicians did not constitute an effective opposition. How could they stand against something that was presented as so appalling? The femicide moral panic gained consensus among the elites and, in response to their demands, new and harsher penalties were introduced by the state.

Helping the weak: the rhetoric of the state close to citizens

Since the early 1990s, profound changes have taken place in the Italian social and political setting. In 1992, at national level a series of judicial inquiries were conducted against politicians and other members of Italian institutions. They revealed a system of corruption and illegal party funding in the form of bribes, with a consequent strong increase in public distrust of the institutions.

From 1994 to 2011, Berlusconi was Prime Minister four times: so-called 'Berlusconism' arose as a social, moral and political phenomenon (Giachetti, 2010; Genovese, 2011). Berlusconism is considered an expression of the crisis of moral values in conjunction with the country's structural crisis (economic, financial, political and institutional). Berlusconi engaged in direct dialogue with the masses and belittled the value of the civil service, institutions and magistrates. His governments promoted large-scale campaigns on the fear of crime, where risks and social anxieties became useful instruments with which to foster insecurity and uncertainty. Hence the state, through its action to protect citizens, and law and safety enforcement, could become reconciled with citizens and also 'converse' with them, thereby providing a representation of the 'state close to citizens'. As Jenkins (1992) suggests, a social, political and economic crisis is a factor that can sometimes engender panics, and the exaggeration of threats is sometimes a strategy to divert attention from a political and economic crisis. Paradoxically, the representations by feminist movements of women and children as vulnerable and victims gave liberal and conservative governments opportunities to reinforce the consensus. Citizens' mistrust of institutions fostered the direct relationship between the charismatic leader (Berlusconi) and the mass, the government and citizens.

The problem of safety (Maneri, 2013) thus became a core issue. The focus on marginal groups, the idea of a society with a high crime rate, the certainty of punishment, harsher sentences and reassurance were strategies and rhetorical instruments with which to govern citizens' mistrust. Paedophilia and femicide were crimes that forcefully entered the discourses on safety. Sensationalism on these themes was easy because they linked with moral and sexual issues.

Berlusconi's scandals disrupted the dialogue and the ideal bond of trust between himself and citizens. The power and dominance of Berlusconi became synonymous with immorality. The sex theme, originated by feminist discourses, became a sensitive topic on which different projects of moralisation (Hunt, 1999) converged and clashed.

As Jenkins argues, social problems and panics are closely connected to each other: a panic is an 'interlinked complex'. 'The continuity of personnel in the claims-making process, the heightened awareness of generalised dangers in the aftermath of a successful panic and the cumulative nature of problem construction' (Jenkins, 1992, p 12) are possible causes of interdependence for the child-abuse moral panic. Otherwise, femicide moral panic seems to utilise a 'socially available knowledge' (Best, 1990): like Berlusconi, men can become (sexual) perverts – corrupt, obscene abusers. Berlusconi became the symbol of immorality and danger. Both the moral panic about child abuse and the moral panic about femicide had feminist roots: children and women were presented as easy victims of the male as predator. The spread of therapy culture in social work (often, again, with its roots in feminist ideas) also played a key part in the development of these moral panics.

Critcher (2003) has argued that moral panics may be seen as either processual or attributional: put simply, in the first model the panic develops through seven stages (emergence, media inventory, moral entrepreneurs, experts, coping and resolution, fade away, legacy), while in the second it needs certain factors to develop (concern, hostility, consensus, disproportionality, volatility, claims makers). My research suggests that both models can be seen in these Italian contemporary moral panics. Consensus and disproportionality are important issues. Consensus appears 'among elites across pressure groups, the media and politicians, initially outside then inside government' (Critcher, 2003, p 150). Consensus is often reached through distortion of the problem, both in disproportionality and in its causes and effects. In the child abuse and femicide moral panics, the threat was exaggerated in the absence of objective measures. The causes and effects of the problems were distorted. Because an organised opposition to this consensus was lacking, and a sufficient level of concern was present, the panics were able to spread.

These moral panics also highlight the issue of the definers. Critcher suggests (2003, p 134) that the explanation offered by Hall et al (1978) is too inflexible, because it considers news sources outside the state as unable to gain credibility. According to Critcher and other authors, media, claims makers and different actors can alternate as primary or secondary definers. I argue that only this latter perspective describes the dynamicity of the situation in which panics develop because, in the moral panics considered, the activism of moral entrepreneurs and interest groups as claims makers should not be under-estimated. Best (1990) suggests that their role is very important in providing a first definition of the problem. Then the media act to amplify problems and concerns, translating them into issues interesting to the public, thus ensuring the latter's constant attention. Finally, the state legitimates these definitions through its responses (changes to the law, campaigns, funds for centres and so on). The state, and not just the media, selects problems and concerns and legitimates those of them that are able to reinforce the image of a state close to citizens and helping the weak. The state is thus a sort of powerful secondary definer with strong power and control over the legitimisation of social concerns, and that contends with the media for second place.

Conclusion: the 'polite state' model

'Women and children first' is an expression that readily demonstrates the symbolic use of weakness by the state. It is a formula that reminds us of the etiquette – the code of behaviour – of civilised society. The state thus becomes symbolically 'polite' to citizens when they are weak and threatened. This image is an icon of Berlusconism (Mariotti, 2011), and the child-abuse moral panic can be viewed as a useful instrument that was used to reinforce this image. The femicide moral panic was different, not least because it emerged following the decay of the Berlusconi era. But the consequences of both are equally profound. A culture of suspicion has arisen in the intimate relationships between children and parents, partners and relatives. This is the culture of the intimate enemy, where distrust is no longer (or not only) in the institutions, but in intimate relationships. Cohen (2011, p 239) comments on such a process:

> The gradual but massive influence of feminism plus the general 'discovery' of the victim created more loops of denunciation, more rules and regulations, more deviance – 'emotional abuse', 'hate crime' and 'sexual harassment' are typical examples – and hence moral panics to be identified and studied.

Child abuse and femicide are two examples of contemporary moral panics that are connected in the Italian social context; the state's complex and controversial role in this is a matter that should not be neglected.

References

Beck, U. (1992) *Risk society: Towards a new modernity*, London and Thousand Oaks: Sage.

Beck, U. and Beck-Gernsheim, E. (1995) *The normal chaos of love*, Cambridge: Polity Press.

Best, J. (1990) *Threatened children: Rhetoric and concern about child victims*, Chicago: University of Chicago Press.

Blumer, H. (1969) *Symbolic interactionism: Perspective and method*, Englewood Cliffs, NJ: Prentice Hall.

Charmaz, K. (2006) *Constructing grounded theory: A practical guide through qualitative analysis*, London: Sage.

Cohen, S. (1972) *Folk devils and moral panics* (3rd edn), London: Routledge, 2002.

Cohen, S. (2011) 'Whose side we were on? The undeclared politics of moral theory', *Crime Media Culture*, vol 7, no 3, pp 237–43.

Critcher, C. (2003) *Moral panics and the media*, London: Open University Press.

Critcher, C. (2009) 'Widening the focus: moral panics as moral regulation', *British Journal of Criminology*, vol 49, no 1, pp 17–34.

de Young, M. (2004) *The day care ritual abuse moral panic,* Jefferson: McFarland.

Furedi, F. (2004) *Therapy culture*, London: Routledge.

Genovese, R. (2011) *Cos'è il berlusconismo: la democrazia deformata e il caso italiano*, Roma: Manifestolibri.

Giachetti, D. (2010) *Berlusconi e il berlusconismo*, Varese: Arterigere.

Giomi, E. and Tonello, F. (2013) 'Women and crime in 365 days of Italian evening news', *Sociologica. Italian Journal of Sociology online*, 3: 1–29, www.sociologica.mulino.it/journal/article/index/Article/Journal:ARTICLE:709/Item/Journal:ARTICLE:709

Goode, E. and Ben-Yehuda, N. (1994) *Moral panics: The social construction of deviance*, Oxford: Blackwell (2nd edn, 2009).

Hall, S., Critcher, C., Jefferson, T., Clarke, J. and Roberts, B. (1978) *Policing the crisis: Mugging, the state and law and order*, London: Macmillan.

Hier, S. (ed) (2011) *Moral panic and the politics of anxiety*, London: Routledge.

Hunt, A. (1999) *Governing morals: A social history of moral regulation*, Cambridge: Cambridge University Press.

James, A., Jenks, C. and Prout, A. (1998) *Theorizing childhood*, Cambridge: Polity Press.

Jenkins, P. (1992) *Intimate enemies: Moral panics in contemporary Great Britain*, New York: Aldine de Gruyter.

Jenkins, P. (1998) *Moral panic: Changing concepts of the child molester in modem America*, New Haven: Yale University Press.

Maneri, M. (2013) 'Si fa presto a dire sicurezza', *Etnografia e ricerca qualitativa*, vol 2, pp 283–309.

Mariotti, C. (2011) 'Berlusconism: some empirical research', *Bulletin of Italian Politics*, vol 3, no 1, pp 35–57.

Russell, D.E.H. and Radford, J. (1992) *Femicide: The politics of woman killing*, New York: Twayne Gale Group.

Tartari, M. (2013) 'Moral panic and ritual abuse. Where's the risk? Findings of an ethnographic research study', in C. Critcher, J. Hughes, J. Petley, and A. Rohloff (eds) *Moral panics in the contemporary world*, New York: Bloomsbury Academic, pp 193–213.

Tartari, M. (2014) 'The ambivalent child. Sexual abuse and representations of childhood inside media and social arenas', *Interdisciplinary Journal of Family Studies*, vol 19, no 1, pp 1–19

Zelizer, V.A. (1994) 'Introduction', in *Pricing the priceless child: The changing social value of children*, Princeton, NJ: Princeton University Press, pp 3–21.

TWO

Myths, monsters and legends: negotiating an acceptable working-class femininity in a marginalised and demonised Welsh locale

Dawn Mannay

Introduction

The distinctiveness of Wales in terms of its political life and culture has grown considerably since the early 2000s (Mackay, 2010). Nevertheless, beneath the imagery of the definitive nation, Wales remains a complex and divided land in which a marginalised and demonised working class has come to characterise areas of Wales dominated by poverty and social exclusion. Such polarisation has a spatial dimension that is illustrated in the creation of new ghettos of prosperity and poverty that now dominate the Welsh socioeconomic terrain, and this 'stigma of place' permeates the identities of residents. The chapter begins by considering how moral panics about particular places create 'spatial folk devils'. The creation of moral panics through political discourses and mediated forms is then explored in terms of contemporary representations. Drawing on research with mothers and their daughters in a marginalised Welsh locale, the chapter examines the ideology of unity alongside the divisions of everyday life, and the ways in which respectable and acceptable working-class femininities are negotiated against a pervasive discourse of lack, stigma and classed moral panics.

Moral panics and folk devils: contemporary representations

As Cohen (1980, p 9) contends, societies are subject to periods of moral panic in which 'a condition, episode, person or group of persons emerges to become defined as a threat to societal values'. Moral panics are often discussed in relation to group criminality, incivility and disorder. However, arguably, the emphasis on collective behaviour has shifted to that of the morality of deficient individuals who require discipline; and these deficiencies are seen as a product of personal choice, where individuals are authors of their own immorality (Burney, 2005). Moral panics are often associated with the sociology of deviance, focusing on 'delinquency, youth cultures, subcultures and style, vandalism, drugs and football hooliganism' (Cohen, 2011, p vi). Nevertheless, the concept of morality also relates to wider discourses about appropriate ways of being that move beyond criminal behaviour and acts of resistance, to encompass socially constructed ideologies that form part of the invisible social order.

The nineteenth century was characterised by moral panics about the ignorance, ineptness and filthiness of working-class women (Delamont, 1978; Aaron et al, 1994; Beddoe, 2000) who were 'defined as a threat to societal values' (Cohen, 1980, p 9). These cultural artefacts of lack remain pervasive in constructions of acceptable working-class femininities; and are remade in current gendered and classed representations of immorality (Mannay and Morgan, 2013; Mannay, 2014). For example, in contemporary moral panics the media have cast working-class mothers as folk devils, responsible for tearing apart the moral fabric of society, where tabloid headlines scream 'family breakdown', 'scroungers' and 'welfare benefit crisis' (Atkinson et al 1998). The figure of 'chav mum' now circulates within a wide range of print media, reality television, news media, films and websites (Tyler, 2008), 'in camouflaged versions of traditional well-known evils' (Cohen, 2011, p viii). Importantly, these representations are always spatialised (Haylett, 2003; Skeggs, 2004), and the narrow sets of discourses and visual tropes that are now drawn upon to portray 'deprived' communities' (Fink and Lomax, 2012) create 'spatial folk devils'. The following section examines how the stigma of place and the creation of 'spatial folk devils' impact on the lives of mothers and daughters who reside in these marginalised areas.

Spatial folk devils: place, space and stigma in urban South Wales

Wales is often presented as a country where locality, community and belonging are of particular importance, but the nation can also be viewed as 'existing in relations of a paradox or antagonism' (Massey, 1994, p 3). Prior to the 1980s, the strength of the Welsh trade union movement contributed to the 'affluent worker' thesis (Adamson, 2010), which has permeated contemporary discourses of ubiquitous classlessness, an idea of shared values and attitudes that allude to a nation where Welshness is inherently working class. However, since 1980 the gap between rich and poor has widened and classlessness has become an imagined concept in a country where the divisions of class are both powerful and pervasive (Evans, 2010). Examining this class divide through geographical distribution illustrates the creation of new ghettos of prosperity and poverty, termed the 'Los Angelization' of socioeconomic terrain (Morrison and Wilkinson, 1995).

This chapter draws on a study[1] that took place in Hystryd,[2] a predominantly white urban area that ranks as one of the most deprived communities in Wales (Welsh Assembly Government, 2008). Nine mothers and their daughters participated in the project and took photographs, drew maps and made collages depicting meaningful places, spaces and activities (see Mannay, 2010; 2013a) and then, drawing on the interpretative model of 'auteur theory' (Rose, 2001), discussed them in individual interviews to ensure that I understood what their visual productions intended to communicate. I have selected data produced with two participants: one mother, Melanie, a mother of two in her thirties, and one daughter, Adele, in her twenties.

These participants were selected as their connections beyond the boundaries of Hystryd act as a constant reminder of how their home is viewed by outsiders. Place is both a heuristic mechanism for placing ourselves and others and a 'social construct arising out of our interactions with others around us' (Scourfield et al, 2006, p 15), but examining the coordinates of mothers' and daughters' social worlds in this study complicates the idea of a single Hystryd. However, the participants are aware of how outsiders view Hystryd in stigmatising and homogenising discourses, and negotiate this ascription in qualitatively different ways.

Melanie's story

Melanie recognises the ways in which her local area is stigmatised and she charts a route to acceptable motherhood and social mobility through her children's education. Faith schools are often seen as vehicles for social mobility (Schagen et al, 2002), and Melanie's project involves attending the church associated with a faith school that is situated in an affluent area outside of Hystryd. Melanie compares attending the church to "going to have a tooth pulled in the dentist", and she describes how she feels in this space outside the boundaries of Hystryd.

> "Women go in hats, and the men, like, go in leather gloves and clip-o-clopity shoes, and they all, you know, they're all perfect, they got their Sunday *best* on (laughs) and then there's me and (partner) in our jeans and (laughs) thinking *oh no argh* ... I mean we're respectable people, you know we're *hard working* and that ... But we're not, *ever* gonna be at a level where, I think some of them in there are.... And even though they're *nice enough*, you know you're never gonna be, *welcomed* as much as anyone else."

Melanie suggests that in the space of the church she becomes what Bauman (1998) refers to as a 'defective consumer', illustrated by the material choices of consumption. The outward differences of apparel are accompanied by an affective realisation of the depth of class division, for although the church constitutionally is open to all, it is as if there is an invisible 'No Entry' sign that mediates the classed nature of this spiritual, religious and social space. The church is situated in an affluent parish outside of Hystryd, and for Melanie this affluence is apparent in the parishioners; she feels that she does not fit in terms of residence or socioeconomic status.

The tension within the space is palpable and Melanie has to negotiate and retain a respectable sense of identity while acknowledging a level of rejection, while members of the congregation may come to feel ill at -ease as they draw from a 'vicarious imagination of the other' (Rock, 2007, p 29) who is entering their space from the 'spatial folk devil' of Hystryd. Melanie adopts strategies of resistance:

> "Sometimes I'm quite hard, and I think *F you, it's for my kids*, I'll sit here and suffer ... Whether you want me here or not ... It's tough."

There is a moral justification for being in this middle-class space, for attending engenders a respectable form of motherhood. As long as Melanie is prepared to leave Hystryd, to enter this affluent parish, she is able to display a normative femininity characterised by her 'capacity to care' (Holloway, 2006). However, the term 'suffer' reinforces Melanie's assertion that she does not want to be in this place, and sufferance also affords a form of self-protection because rejection is more palatable if you can reject the other. Thus, as Bennett et al (2008) suggest, detachment is a better notion than exclusion, but, despite Melanie's bravado, entering and re-entering this space is emotionally wearing, with the pain of continual perceptions, assumptions and judgements that question the legitimacy of the family marked by their Hystryd postcode as defective (Rogaly and Taylor, 2009; Skeggs, 2009).

Adele's story

In common with many working-class students (Ball et al, 2002), Adele attends a local university so that she can commute from home, and this journey engenders a recognition of the stigmatised discourses that surround her home. As discussed elsewhere (Mannay, 2013b), as a 'non-traditional' student Adele is negotiating a hybrid identity as she moves constantly between two qualitatively different spaces, and, like Melanie, she makes distinctions between herself and her more affluent peers:

> "Because I live at home it was like I wasn't, didn't really get on, not get on with them but I wasn't part of them ... like their parents are paying for them to come to uni ... And like half of them haven't even got jobs."

'Working' is central to working-class respectability. Those who 'haven't even got jobs' may have financial superiority, but Adele still retains a moral high ground because such students can be seen as a type of 'benefit person', and Adele, who worked as soon as she was old enough, "wasn't part of them". The same moral justifications and distinctions can be seen in relation to cleanliness: "I'm not like, I couldn't live in a student, like in the mess ... I couldn't do it."

Dirt forms a symbolic nexus from which working-class women struggle to disassociate (Evans, 2006), and Adele employs these distinctions to explain why she is not like the other students and why she does not socialise with them outside of university. However, as mentioned in relation to Melanie's account, detachment is a better notion than exclusion (Bennett et al, 2008), and such separation may also be engendered to limit any opportunities for her peers to make judgements about Hystryd and, in turn, her marked identity. In a discussion about a university field-trip where they passed through a low-income area that was ridiculed by Adele's peers, I asked Adele if any of the students knew where she lived:

> "No they don't even know 'cause they're not from here ...
> I think they'd probably, if they drove through here I think they'd probably have a heart attack. (laughs) (both laugh)"

In this way, Adele acknowledges Hystryd as a 'spatialised folk devil' and, although there is laughter, her account also suggests an element of concealment engendered as a protective force against being fixed as the object of comedy (Tyler, 2008) or being wounded by lack of respect (Bennett et al, 2008).

Discussion

The notion that everyone who lives in a 'spatial folk devil' like Hystryd must be a dysfunctional disaster from some underclass has lodged deep in the local social mythology. Stigma of place impacts on everyday lives, perceptions of others and perceptions of self. It can close down projects of social mobility and engender divided communities and divided selves. This feeds into a process of social spatialisation where residents are subject to the over-simplification, stereotyping and labelling that equates home, and simultaneously them, as something to be judged as deficient and 'defined as a threat to societal values' (Cohen, 1980, p 9).

As Thrift (1997, p 160) contends, 'places form a reservoir of meanings which people can draw upon to tell stories about and therefore define themselves'; and both Melanie and Adele are acutely aware of how they are stigmatised. The readings of families relate to who they are in regard to their postcode, so that they are never allowed to forget where they live; and conceptions of place are guided by moral panics around sink estates, where locals become coded by their residence in the 'next-door yet foreign place where the other neighbours live' (Toynbee, 2003, p 19). Accordingly, particular housing areas like Hystryd become 'spatial folk devils' and residents are ascribed with this marked identity that impacts on the practices and power relations that define their everyday lives

This does not mean that marginalised areas do not experience problems; as Blanford (2010) argues, parts of South Wales, still badly affected by deindustrialisation, are very difficult places to grow up in, as is demonstrated in the participants' accounts. However, central to all moral panics and their associated folk devils is that the issue's 'extent and significance has been exaggerated' (Cohen, 2011, p vii) in relation to either more reliable forms of evidence or other more serious social problems. Such exaggeration has altered the range of ways in which particular areas can be seen from both inside and outside, so that Melanie and Adele need to negotiate acceptable femininities against pervasive and vehement discourses of lack, disorder and the caricature of the 'chav mum' (Aaron, 1994; Tyler, 2008).

Conclusion

This chapter has reflected on the historical classed and gendered legacies that engender the creation of folk devils and has presented contemporary evidence to demonstrate the ways in which these folk devils are made, remade and circulated in the media. Drawing on the accounts of Melanie and Adele, the chapter has illustrated the affective impact of residing in a marginalised and stigmatised locale. Both Melanie and Adele employ strategies of resistance as they embark on educational projects of social mobility, but these journeys are undertaken with the recognition of stigma, the need to continually re-establish a moral sense of self, acts of necessary concealment and emotional costs; as Melanie says, "it's tough".

Acknowledgements

I would like to acknowledge the participants who made this article possible, and also Professor John Fitz, Professor Emma Renold and Dr Bella Dicks for supervising this research project. I am grateful to Professor Viviene Cree, Dr Gary Clapton and Dr Mark Smith for inviting me to contribute to this edited collection. Lastly, I would like to thank Dr Sara Delamont, whose anthropology module Myths, Monsters and Legends inspired the title of this chapter and who has been a continual source of support in my academic writing.

Notes

[1] The doctoral research project from which this paper is drawn was titled 'Mothers and daughters on the margins: gender, generation and education' and was funded by the Economic and Social Research Council.

[2] The name Hystryd is fictitious and was chosen to maintain the anonymity of the area.

References

Aaron, J. (1994) 'Finding a voice in two tongues: gender and colonization', in J. Aaron, T. Rees, S. Betts and M. Vincentelli (eds) *Our sisters' land: The changing identities of women in Wales*, Cardiff: University of Wales Press.

Aaron, J., Rees, T., Betts, S. and Vincentelli, M. (1994) *Our sisters' land: The changing identities of women in Wales*, Cardiff: University of Wales Press.

Adamson, D. (2010) 'Work', in H. Mackay (ed) *Understanding contemporary Wales*, Milton Keynes: The Open University and University of Wales Press, pp 59–90.

Atkinson, K., Oerton, S. and Burns, D. (1998) 'Happy families? Single mothers, the press and the politicians', *Capital & Class*, vol 22, no 1, pp 1–11.

Ball, S.J., Reay, D. and David, M. (2002) 'Ethnic choosing: minority ethnic students, social class and higher education choice', *Race, Ethnicity and Education*, vol 5, no 4, pp 333–57.

Bauman, Z. (1998) *Work, consumerism and the new poor*, Buckingham: Open University Press.

Beddoe, D. (2000) *Out of the shadows: A history of women in twentieth-century Wales*, Cardiff: University of Wales Press.

Bennett, T., Savage, M., Silva, E., Warde, A., Gayo-Cal, M. and Wright, D. (2008) *Culture, class, distinction*, Abingdon: Routledge.

Blanford, S. (2010) 'Cultural representation', in H. Mackay (ed) *Understanding contemporary Wales*, Milton Keynes: Open University and University of Wales Press.

Burney, E. (2005) *Making people behave*, Cullompton: Willan.

Cohen, S. (1980) *Folk devils and moral panics*, London: Routledge.

Cohen, S. (2011) *Folk devils and moral panics*, London: Routledge.

Delamont, S. (1978) 'The domestic ideology and women's education', in S. Delamont and L. Duffin (eds) *The nineteenth century woman*, London: Routledge, pp 134–63.

Evans, G. (2006) *Educational failure and working class white children in Britain*, London: Palgrave Macmillan.

Evans, N. (2010) 'Class', in H. Mackay (ed) *Understanding contemporary Wales*, Milton Keynes: The Open University and University of Wales Press, pp 125–58.

Fink, J. and Lomax, H. (2012) 'Inequalities, images and insights for policy and research', *Critical Social Policy*, vol 32, no 1, pp 3–10.

Haylett, C. (2003) 'Culture, class and urban policy: reconsidering equality', *Antipode*, vol 35, no 1, pp 33–55.

Holloway, W. (2006) *The capacity to care: Gender and ethical subjectivity*, London: Routledge.

Mackay, H. (2010) 'Rugby – an introduction to contemporary Wales', in H. Mackay (ed) *Understanding contemporary Wales*, Milton Keynes: The Open University.

Mannay, D. (2010) 'Making the familiar strange: can visual research methods render the familiar setting more perceptible?', *Qualitative Research*, vol 10, no 1, pp 91–111.

Mannay, D. (2013a) '"Who put that on there … why why why?" Power games and participatory techniques of visual data production', *Visual Studies*, vol 28, no 2, pp 136–46.

Mannay, D. (2013b) 'Keeping close and spoiling revisited: exploring the significance of "home" for family relationships and educational trajectories in a marginalised estate in urban south Wales', *Gender and Education*, vol 25, no 1, pp 91–107.

Mannay, D. (2014) 'Who should do the dishes now? Exploring gender binaries around housework in contemporary urban south Wales', *Contemporary Wales*, vol 27, no 1, pp 21–39.

Mannay, D. and Morgan, M. (2013) 'Anatomies of inequality: considering the emotional cost of aiming higher for marginalised, mature mothers re-entering education', *Journal of Adult and Continuing Education*, vol 19, no 1, pp 57–75.

Massey, D. (1994) *Space, place, and gender*, Minneapolis, MN: University of Minnesota Press.

Morrison, J. and Wilkinson, B. (1995) 'Poverty and prosperity in Wales: polarization and Los Angelization', *Contemporary Wales* vol 8, pp 29–45.

Rock, P. (2007) 'Symbolic interactionism and ethnography', in P. Atkinson, A. Coffey, S. Delamont, J. Lofland and L. Lofland (eds) *Handbook of ethnography*, London: Sage, pp 26–38.

Rogaly, B. and Taylor, B. (2009) *Moving histories of class and community*, London: Palgrave.

Rose, G. (2001) *Visual methodologies*, London: Sage.

Schagen, S., Davies, D., Rudd, P. and Schagen, I. (2002) *The impact of specialist and faith schools on performance*, LGA Research Report 28, Slough: National Foundation for Educational Research.

Scourfield, J., Dicks, B., Drakeford, M. and Davies, A. (2006) *Children, place and identity*, London: Routledge.

Skeggs, B. (2004) *Class, self and culture*, London: Routledge.

Skeggs, B. (2009) 'Haunted by the spectre of judgement: respectability, value and affect in class relations', in K.P. Sveinsson (ed) *Who cares about the white working class?* London: Runnymede Trust, pp 36–45.

Thrift, N. (1997) 'Us and them: reimagining places, reimagining identities', in H. Mackay (ed) *Consumption and everyday life*, London: Sage, pp 159–212.

Toynbee, P. (2003) *Hard work: Life in low pay Britain*, London: Bloomsbury.

Tyler, I. (2008) 'Chav mum chav scum', *Feminist Media Studies*, vol 8, no 1, pp 17–34.

Welsh Assembly Government (2008) *Welsh index of multiple deprivation 2008*, Cardiff: Welsh Assembly Government.

THREE

Making a moral panic: 'feral families', family violence and welfare reforms in New Zealand. Doing the work of the state?

Liz Beddoe

Introduction

New Zealand is in the midst of a campaign to cut welfare spending, aligned to the 'austerity' discourse preoccupying many countries. Over the period 2011–14, two significant government projects were developed side by side: a programme of welfare reforms (Welfare Working Group, 2011) and a new programme of interventions aimed at reducing the incidence of child abuse (Ministry of Social Development (MSD), 2012b). The two projects emanated from the same arm of government, the MSD, but they were not linked in their everyday activities. Both projects have generated significant public interest and are imbued with ideological content.

Negative framing of the poor – alongside amplified expressions of class disgust – amid the on-going programme of welfare reform has been noted elsewhere (Tyler, 2013). Links between child maltreatment and welfare claimants are also common (Warner, 2013). An analysis of the media discourse on welfare families in New Zealand has found significant linking of family violence to poverty and 'beneficiary' or claimant status, most noticeable in examination of the commentary on 'opinion pieces' or columns. A battle of words rages between advocacy groups (Wynd, 2013) that research poverty in New Zealand and those who would link the issue of 'welfare families' to child abuse and neglect.

This chapter explores the construction of a 'feral families' discourse in the New Zealand print media and considers whether this construction may constitute an example of the 'folk devil' so often manifest in a moral panic. Such families are characterised as being welfare dependent, prone to violence and predominantly Maori.

Framing of the poor

In all discussions of moral panics, the role of the media is germane. Iyengar (1990, p 19) argued that 'how people think about poverty is shown to be dependent on how the issue is framed'. Iyengar's influential paper on media framing associates the psychological conception of framing – ideas and terms employed to propose and consider choices – to the way mass media influence public opinion on the major social issues. In contemporary society 'media' is no longer a monolithic category. While the press and broadcast media may maintain significant influence on the framing of social problems, they are also subject to immediate challenge. A good recent example is the tranche of opinions of citizens, politicians and journalists that followed the screening of the television programme *Benefits Street* (Channel Four, 2014). The highly controversial documentary about the residents of a street in England elicited instant reactions in social media, followed up by stories, blogs and further television coverage. At one end of the spectrum of comments, residents were subjected to abuse and threats; at the other, there was nuanced discussion of how the programme framed the poor, essentially illustrating polarised opinions about the provision of welfare. This example demonstrates that although news and other media can fan the flames of moral panics, the audience is no longer passive, nor denied opportunities to stake a claim in the debates.

Gamson's (1992) constructionist approach to framing is useful, as it underlines the importance of audience engagement in interpreting media discourses; indeed, 'media discourses and public opinion are conceived to be two interacting systems' (Sotirovic, 2000, p 273) and journalists must condense all the available information into essential ideas or frames. Thus, in the example given above, journalists and commentators took standpoints, positioning themselves either as defenders of the documentary or as advocates for those participants deemed to be defamed by the programme. Gamson (1992) suggested that the success of media framing is influenced by the strategies employed by audiences: those people who use a cultural strategy (received wisdom, 'common sense', stereotypes and so forth) may be more impacted on by framing, while those with 'personal or vicarious experiential knowledge' are more likely to discount or ignore frames (Sotirovic, p 274). Such is the power of the audience that the residents of *Benefits Street* were allowed the right of reply: a programme screened after the final episode (Plunkett, 2014). Media framing is still potent, for while technology mediates reception of the news, unsympathetic media hostile to particular groups can exploit stigma.

Public reactions to social problems addressed in mainstream media issues reflect deeply held ideologies, preferences and prior judgements; words or phrases may trigger ideological and emotional responses. An audience may be unwilling to allow framing to alter their views, once that emotional response is triggered. Language is significant, and Bullock, Fraser Wyche and Williams (2001, p 233) have argued that along with 'rhetorical devices such as metaphors, catch phrases and imagery, news-handlers use reasoning devices that draw on causal attributions ... These powerful (but typically unnoticed) mechanisms affect viewers' judgments of responsibility and causality.' As noted by Sotirovic (2000, p 272), in the 'quest for a catchy phrase, welfare mothers became "welfare queens" ... welfare recipients became "welfare freeloaders" hiding the reality of illiteracy, abuse, illnesses, and addictions'. Whatever the motivations of the *Benefits Street* documentary makers, the television channel set the tone with the title, summoning a discourse bound to attract a large audience in 'austerity Britain'. The public is invited into the lives of people to assess their deservedness.

It has been noted in the UK, as elsewhere, that in the 'age of austerity' a common element of the discourse is the labelling of 'feckless' parents 'as scapegoats for moral and economic decline' (Jensen and Tyler, 2012). In New Zealand, there is evidence of moral framing of Maori (indigenous people of New Zealand) families and welfare beneficiary status, as shown in the following media story, linking child-abuse statistics to the beneficiary status of teen parents:

> "So it's not just a Maori problem, it's a New Zealand problem, and they are not the only ones that abuse their children but they are disproportionately high" ... Teenage parents were the most vulnerable group, Minister Bennett [MSD] said. About 4500 babies were born every year to teenagers receiving a benefit and 45 per cent would have another child while still on a benefit, she said. (Stuff [online news website], 26 July 2011)

Maori comprised nearly 15% (598,602 people) of the population of New Zealand in the 2013 census (Statistics New Zealand, 2014). The Maori population is youthful, with the 2013 census reporting that (33.1%) of people of Maori descent were aged under 15 years (Statistics New Zealand, 2014), and as compared with other children in New Zealand Maori children are over-represented in rates of child maltreatment (Cooper and Wharewera-Mika, 2013). While this is acknowledged as a significant problem to be addressed, it must be recognised that by far the majority of Maori children are well cared for (Cooper and Wharewera-Mika, 2013).

Cooper and Wharewera-Mika note that numerous historical sources such as early settler accounts of Maori family life reported supportive and warm child-raising practices (Cooper and Wharewera-Mika, 2013, p 170). When seeking understanding of the over-representation of Maori children in family violence, the persistent theme concerns colonisation and the subsequent enduring inequalities. The process of colonisation caused significant loss of land, severe erosion of language and traditional cultural practices and the breakdown of indigenous systems of community norms and justice. These losses are widely acknowledged as having a negative effect on Maori culture, health and overall socioeconomic well-being (Durie, 2001; Kruger et al, 2004). Kruger et al (2004, p 29) state that 'epidemic whanau violence and systemic dysfunction' is an outcome of persistent oppression and inequality.

While child maltreatment is recognised as a major challenge, Maori people appear to be targeted for particular vilification and association with the discourses of underclass and 'feral families' (Laws, 2012a). The entrepreneur of such a discourse can and will attempt to silence other voices by undermining their credibility or accusing them of some form of neglect:

> Children's Commissioner Cindy Kiro will wring her hands and preach that 'we' must stop harming 'our' kids but the truth remains. Being born to an underclass family, especially if you are Maori, increases the risk of child abuse and child murder by an exponential degree.... Again we will hear excuses and blame-shifting from the liberal apologists ... (Laws, 2008)

In the local manifestation, 'welfare-dependent families' have also been labelled as 'feral' and an emerging highly racialised underclass discourse is revealed and repeatedly linked to family violence:

> The children of welfare are now legion, and they are destined for the same lifestyle as their, usually, solo parent. They smoke, drink, drug, crime, victim, bash like no other group in the country. And then they breed some more. (Laws, 2008)

The folk devil: the construct of 'feral Maori families'

The elements of Cohen's original definition of a moral panic are: a 'condition, episode, person or group of persons' emerges as a potential threat to society; the nature of the threat is presented as a stylised or stereotypical version of itself by the media (the 'folk devil'); moral entrepreneurs and 'experts' present this threat and possible solutions to the public and, lastly, the threat then disappears and is forgotten, or deteriorates and becomes more visible, often being institutionalised in some lasting way (Cohen, 2002, p 1). The 'folk devil' is generally depicted by the media in an easily recognised form (Thompson, 1998, p 8) and the threat is generally not to something trivial, but to something that is integral to the society in question (Thompson, 1998, p 8).

In the introduction to the third edition of *Folk Devils and Moral Panics*, Cohen considers that the objects of moral panics are both 'new' threats and manifestations of old threats (Cohen, 2002, p vii); they are damaging per se and also symptomatic of deeper problems (Cohen, 2002, p viii); and they are at once transparent and opaque, easily recognisable, but in need of explanation to the public by 'experts' (Cohen, 2002, p viii). Stories of family violence, in particular of child abuse, are often couched in terms of moral degeneration, what can be coded as 'a world gone mad', framed as phenomena symptomatic of the decline of modern society. This decline is often attributed to the stigmatised other – those who are poor, immigrants, members of ethnic and religious communities, welfare beneficiaries – and is the beloved target of the right-wing blogger, 'do-gooder liberals' and academics. The 'bleeding hearts' are seen by the powerful to coalesce around an unreasonable defence of those held responsible for the decline.

Moral panics ideas are useful in exploring the role of claims makers in the discourse of the 'feral' Maori family. It can be argued that the news media is playing a role in bolstering fear and social anxiety about the presence and impact of 'dangerous' welfare-dependent Maori families and communities. Does this suggest that we have a moral panic, where framing has created a unique folk-devil, tapping into the vein of racism that exists in New Zealand society? My answer is both yes and no. Yes, because the promotion of a racist discourse sits alongside the neoliberal state project of cutting benefits to many vulnerable people on quasi-moral grounds, and thus potentially giving support to those who sponsor the welfare-reform agenda. The framing of a racialised underclass discourse, with a 'bonus' link to child maltreatment, may bolster the New Zealand government's social policy direction by permeating the public consciousness with such a negative portrayal. No, because there is also some evidence that these views are at the extreme end of a continuum and not widely shared in New Zealand society. I also feel that the notion of 'feral Maori families' is a racist trope too offensive to attract the more socially acceptable moral entrepreneur who might be needed to justify this discourse as in itself constituting a moral panic.

It is useful to explore the manifestation of such a discourse here. In New Zealand, politician and columnist Michael Laws wrote a series of articles over 2008–12 in which he addressed 'feral families', more commonly just referring to his subjects as 'the ferals'. That the feral Maori family folk devil has some potency is evidenced in online comments. Abusive language and racist stereotypes abound, often always interwoven with gender and class labels. While Laws was not the only commentator drawing on racialised underclass discourse, he was perhaps the most prolific and vitriolic. In an article entitled 'The inevitable result of a boy born bad', reporting on a young male arrested for a serious sexual assault on a child, Laws wrote of

> that sub-species of humanity with which we co-exist
> – the ferals. These evolutionary antisocials have created
> their own nihilist culture and provide 90 per cent of this
> country's social problems. They have core characteristics
> that distinguish them: poor education, transience, a
> dependence upon drink and/or drugs, a criminal history,
> a welfare lifestyle and they are disproportionately Maori.
> (Laws, 2012a)

Later in 2012, Laws' column 'The Tragic Life of JJ Lawrence' referred to the death of a toddler, but he reserved his personal acrimony for the mother:

> All the usual ingredients are present: ethnicity, welfare
> dependence, drugs, previous violence and the feral
> boyfriend. But there is another ingredient that we often
> overlook – the feckless and useless mother who sets up
> her child for harm ... simple messages can go out now

– and especially to Maori mothers ... If you can't handle
the job, stop breeding. (Laws, 2012b)

Other newspaper columnists have attempted to invoke the 'troubled
families' approach. For example, Dita De Boni writes, 'Where social
services, the police and many others are involved with a family, it
doesn't seem to prevent a big tragedy occurring – even when the
family is known to be a wellspring of trouble.' In introducing the UK
'Troubled Families' scheme, she notes 'An ex-crime reporter once
told me that police had told her that in any given community, there
will be a handful of families that cause the majority of trouble – and
cost to the taxpayer' (De Boni, 2011) . She then mentions five cases
of child abuse, all involving Maori families. This New Zealand media
framing has been analysed in detail by Provan (2012, p 202), who
noted that 'murdered Maori children are more likely to be named in
a "roll of dishonour", thus framing family violence as solely a Maori
problem'. A further attack on Maori is then rendered palatable. Du
Fresne (2010) criticises Maori leaders for preferring to spend their
time reminding Pakeha (European New Zealanders) of the impact
of colonisation rather 'than grappling with the ugly reality of Maori
violence', and thus attempts to extinguish an accepted analysis of the
historical trauma, the 'multiple and compounded layers of pain, grief
and loss experienced by indigenous people since European contact'
(Freeman, 2007, p 108).

Those presenting a more nuanced and sympathetic view of child
poverty, for example Freeth (2013), who called on business people to
contribute more, face a barrage of critical comments, including this:

A quarter of all Kiwi children are raised in families ...
where cigarettes, alcohol, gambling and drugs come first.
Three generations of state sponsored dysfunction has made
these families a costly blight on the working/middle class
... Is it time for a few draconian laws to clean the gutters
and reduce the pests? (*New Zealand Herald*, Comment, 6
March 2013)

Such an invocation of eugenic arguments accompanies welfare reforms that have heralded greater surveillance and control of those claiming benefits. Such policy reflects the moral framing intrinsic to policy development. In New Zealand the Future Focus policy introduced in 2010 is an approach that requires sole parents on the Domestic Purposes Benefit (DPB) to be in part-time work once the youngest child turns six (Ministry of Social Development, 2010). Failure to conform incurs sanctions that are outlined in the Social Security (New Work Tests, Incentives, and Obligations) Amendment Act 2010. Further reforms in 2012 included requiring sole parents on the DPB who decide to have another child while on DPB to return to work after the child's first birthday. One policy that caused much critical comment was that mothers on DPB and their daughters will be offered free contraception to prevent pregnancies that may lead to their having to leave the work-force (Trevett, 2012). In addition, beneficiaries must enrol their pre-schoolers with a general practitioner and complete health checks. Children aged 3 must attend 15 hours a week of early childhood education. Failure to comply results in the sanction of a 50% benefit cut (Ministry of Social Development, 2012a).

Conclusions

Wacquant (2009, p 100) argued that in both the criminal and welfare systems 'public vilification racial accentuation and even inversion, and moral individuation work in tandem to make punitive programs the policy tool of choice and censorious condemnation the central public rationale' for the implementation of more punitive justice and welfare programmes. New Zealand is not alone in its examples of the framing of welfare-claimant folk devils alongside a political platform of stringent welfare reforms. While in New Zealand claims makers such as media commentators have clearly employed a central device of moral panic, identifying targets that are easily amplified as folk devils, this has not produced the 'screaming' headlines observed elsewhere. Is there hope, then, that the public might reject the most draconian reforms, despite the potent imagery of evil, feral, dysfunctional 'welfare families'? New

Zealand has a history of investing in social development policies to develop community responses to intransigent problems such as child abuse and health inequality, and this has included specific policies to develop community capacity (see, for example, Humpage, 2005; Elizabeth and Larner, 2009). As such, the claim of a world over-run by dangerous 'welfare dependent' families must be examined critically against some evidence that New Zealanders resist an extreme form of welfare reform (Humpage, 2011), thus failing to produce the volatility of a classic moral panic.

References

Bullock, H.E., Fraser Wyche, K. and Williams, W.R. (2001) 'Media images of the poor', *Journal of Social Issues*, vol 57, no 2, pp 229–46.

Channel Four (2014) 'Benefits Street', www.channel4.com/ programmes/benefits-street (accessed 17 January 2014).

Cohen, S. (2002) *Folk devils and moral panics* (3rd edn), London: Routledge.

Cooper, E. and Wharewera-Mika, J. (2013) 'Healing: towards and understanding of Maori child mistreatment', in T. McIntosh and M. Mulholland (eds), *Maori and Social Issues*, vol 1, Wellington: Huia, pp 169–86.

De Boni, D. (2011) 'Our unruly families', *New Zealand Herald* (12 December).

Du Fresne, K. (2010) 'Reveal-all culture undermines bounds of bad behaviour', *Dominion Post* (12 October).

Durie, M. (2001) *Mauri ora: The dynamics of Maori health*, Auckland: Oxford University Press.

Elizabeth, V. and Larner, W. (2009) 'Racializing the "Social development" state: investing in children in Aotearoa/New Zealand, *Social Politics: International Studies in Gender, State & Society*, vol 16, no 1, pp 132–58.

Freeman, B. (2007) 'Indigenous pathways to anti-oppressive practice', in D. Baines (ed) *Doing anti-oppressive practice*, Halifax, NS: Fernwood, pp 95–110.

Freeth, A. (2013) 'The sad business of child poverty: businesses cannot sit on hands while children go hungry, uneducated, abused and neglected', *New Zealand Herald* (6 March).

Gamson, W.A. (1992) *Talking politics*, Cambridge, England: Cambridge University Press.

Humpage, L. (2005) 'Experimenting with a "whole of government" approach: indigenous capacity building in New Zealand and Australia', *Policy Studies*, vol 26, no 1, pp 47–66.

Humpage, L. (2011) 'What do New Zealanders think about welfare?' *Policy Quarterly*, vol 7, no 2, pp 8–13.

Iyengar, S. (1990) 'Framing responsibility for political issues: the case of poverty', *Political Behavior*, vol 12, no 1, pp 19–40.

Jensen, T. and Tyler, I. (2012) 'Austerity parenting: new economies of parent-citizenship', *Studies in the Maternal*, vol 4, no 2.

Kruger, T., Pitman, M., Grennell, D., McDonald, T., Mariu, D., Pomare, A., Mita, T., Maihi, M. and Lawson-Te Aho, K. (2004) *Transforming whanau violence: A conceptual framework*, Wellington: Te Puni Kokiri-Second Maori Taskforce on Whanau Violence.

Laws, M. (2008) 'Child abuse symptom of human race evolving into them and us', *Sunday Star Times* (27 December).

Laws, M. (2012a) 'The inevitable result of a boy born bad', *Christchurch Press* (4 March).

Laws, M. (2012b) 'The tragic life of JJ Lawrence', *Sunday Star Times* (18 November).

Ministry of Social Development (2010) *Future Focus changes to the welfare system*, Wellington: NZ Government.

Ministry of Social Development (2012a) *Welfare Reform Paper E: Social obligations for parents*, Wellington: NZ Government.

Ministry of Social Development (2012b) *White Paper on Vulnerable Children*, Wellington: NZ Government.

Plunkett, J. (2014) 'Benefits Street: residents to get the right of reply in live TV debate', *Guardian* (online) (16 January), www.theguardian.com/media/2014/jan/16/benefits-street-residents-live-broadcast

Provan, S. (2012) *The uncanny place of the bad mother and the innocent child at the heart of New Zealand's 'cultural identity'*, New Zealand: University of Canterbury Christchurch, http://hdl.handle.net/10092/7393.

Sotirovic, M. (2000) 'Effects of media use on audience framing and support for welfare', *Mass Communication and Society*, vol 3, nos 2–3, pp 269–96, doi: 10.1207/s15327825mcs0323_06.

Statistics New Zealand (2014) 2013 Census ethnic group profiles: Maori, www.stats.govt.nz/Census/2013-census/profile-and-summary-reports/ethnic-profiles.

Stuff.co.nz (2011) 'Maori child abuse disproportionately high: Minister' (26 July), www.stuff.co.nz/national/politics/5338700/Maori-child-abuse-disproportionately-high-Minister

Thompson, K. (1998) *Moral panics*, London: Routledge.

Trevett, C. (2012) 'Free birth control for beneficiaries', *The New Zealand Herald, Online* (8 May), www.nzherald.co.nz/nz/news/article.cfm?c_id=1&objectid=10804206

Tyler, I. (2013) *Revolting subjects: Social abjection and resistance in neoliberal Britain*, London: Zed Books.

Wacquant, L. (2009) *Punishing the poor: The neoliberal government of social insecurity*, Durham, NC: Duke University Press.

Warner, J. (2013) 'Social work, class politics and risk in the moral panic over Baby P', *Health, Risk & Society*, vol 15, no 3, pp 217–33.

Welfare Working Group (2011) *Reducing long-term benefit dependency: Recommendations,* Wellington: Institute of Policy Studies.

Wynd, D. (2013) *Child abuse: What role does poverty play?* Auckland: Child Poverty Action Group.

FOUR

The wrong type of mother: moral panic and teenage parenting

Sally Brown

Introduction

In many Western countries where teenage pregnancy rates are considered by policy makers and others to be too high, such as the UK, USA and Canada, governments have made concerted efforts to reduce teenage pregnancies (for example, Social Exclusion Unit, 1999), while a considerable body of research into the lived experiences of teenage parents has built up (for example, Kirkman et al, 2001; Geronimus, 2003; Whitley and Kirmayer, 2008). In earlier decades, becoming pregnant as a teenager was most likely to be seen as a moral problem due to the mother-to-be being unmarried, and that was often swiftly solved by marriage to the young father-to-be. In more recent years, the 'problem' has been relabelled as a social one, mainly as part of a discourse about social exclusion, and in health terms, as a discourse about risks to both mother and child.

However, despite this shift to regarding teenage pregnancy and parenting as social and health problems, the moral overtones have not gone away, and, it could be argued, have resurfaced in recent years. For example, when the Conservative leader David Cameron harangued the UK parliament at Prime Minister's Question Time in 2008 about the death of Peter Connelly, he did so on the (false) premise that Peter's mother was a teenage mother; this was, as he presented it, all the evidence that was needed of her guilt. Since then, a sense of moral panic about welfare benefit scroungers has been promulgated by the

UK's Coalition government as part of its austerity agenda, and young parents have been positioned, implicitly and indeed explicitly, among the ranks of the scroungers. This link between pervasive stereotypes of teen parents dependent on benefits and the ideological assumption that early child-bearing stems from poor individual choices and lifestyles has a direct (and negative) impact on young parents' well-being.

This chapter will first outline the connections between the austerity agenda, young parents and moral panic, using the model of moral panics developed by Goode and Ben-Yehuda (1994) as a framework for analysis. It will then present findings from recent research in which young parents discussed the stigmatisation they experience, and their resulting self-surveillance as a response to their perceptions about constantly being judged by people around them. The chapter will conclude by discussing how young parents both acknowledge and resist the stigmatising discourse of moral panics around teenage pregnancy and parenting.

Teenage parenting as a moral panic

Goode and Ben-Yehuda (1994) argue that a moral panic exists when a substantial proportion of a population regard a particular subgroup as posing a threat to society and moral order as a result of their behaviour, and demand that something must be done – that something often being 'strengthening the social control apparatus of society' (Goode and Ben-Yehuda, 1994, p 31). They argue that there are five crucial criteria for a moral panic: concern, hostility, consensus, disproportionality and volatility. Turning to the issue of teenage pregnancy and parenthood, in this case-study example we can see evidence of *concern* in that anxiety is sparked by what is presented in the media as large numbers of teenagers having babies, particularly when compared to other European countries, and this is described as a threat to the fabric of the community and the institution of the family. Concern is also present in terms of the harms that are said to be caused, to both mothers and babies, by teenage pregnancy and parenting, and therefore 'something must be done' to stop babies being born into circumstances that, it is claimed, will lead to their growing up disadvantaged from the start. There is evidence of *hostility* to the teenagers, in terms of portraying them as 'folk devils' who want to get 'something for nothing', particularly in the context of a rhetoric about benefit 'scroungers', and also in terms of stories being told, for example, about teenagers getting pregnant in order to get a council flat ahead of other more 'deserving' cases. There is *consensus* about this being a problem, seen in the broad negative social reaction in speeches by politicians and stories in the popular press. The size of the problem is exaggerated, as demonstrated by the data discussed below, thus demonstrating *disproportionality*; and we can see *volatility* in the way the problem emerges suddenly, and may disappear just as quickly. One interesting aspect of teenage pregnancy as a moral panic is the way it emerges, disappears and then re-emerges, never quite going away completely, although the social and political context might be subtly different in each iteration. Garland (2008) reminds us that there is always a *moral dimension* to the social reaction, which can be seen in statements from politicians and the press relating to the family, particularly about 'Broken Britain' and on-going fears about the 'breakdown of the family'. That the 'deviant conduct' in question is seen as *symptomatic* of wider problems within society is demonstrated by, for example, Prime Minister David Cameron's linking of poor parenting to social unrest (Cabinet Office, 2011a), or using a single mother with a pregnant teenager as one of his examples justifying the introduction of the 'Troubled Families' initiative (Cabinet Office, 2011b).

As for the true scale of the problem, according to the Office for National Statistics (2011) the teenage birth rate has been falling steadily for 30 years, and in 2010 was at its lowest point since 1968. In addition, conception rates increased in all age groups excepting the under-20s; in other words, fewer teenagers are getting pregnant, and fewer of those who do get pregnant are carrying the baby to term. However, in order to have a moral panic, people must believe that there is something to panic about and, despite these figures, a survey conducted in 2013 in the UK found that people think teenage pregnancy is about 25 times higher than it actually is: the survey showed that people think 15% of under-16s get pregnant every year when official figures suggest it is about 0.6% (Ipsos-MORI, 2013). Lawlor and Shaw (2004) argue that:

> Health professionals and the general public should be wary of claims that the rate of teenage pregnancy in Britain is 'high' and increasing in an alarming way. International comparisons suggest that the rate is moderate and that the past six decades have seen a decline rather than a rise…. We believe that the selective reporting of international and time comparisons by policy makers results in a 'manufactured risk' and has more to do with moral panic than public health. (Lawlor and Shaw, 2004, p 123)

As far as welfare benefits are concerned, the Coalition government's welfare reforms will mean that parents under the age of 25 years will have their benefits reduced, and UK Prime Minister David Cameron has suggested that under-25s should have no rights to housing benefit at all, meaning that young parents would find it very difficult to live independently, as they are likely to be in low-paid work, and in need of housing benefit even if they are in work. The age range of the parents targeted by the reforms signals a widening scope of concern to include parents in the first half of their 20s, a broadening of the concept of 'young' that appears to reflect largely middle- and upper-class views about acceptable life-course transitions. This discourse is one where education and career are prioritised, with child-bearing being delayed until a career is established, as the preferred life course, and early motherhood is positioned as undesirable, if not irresponsible (Perrier, 2013; Wilson and Huntington, 2005).

Changes to the benefits system have been linked to the increasing stigmatisation of benefit claimants, including the use of increasingly harsh language to describe some groups (Garthwaite, 2011) and an assumption promoted by some sections of the media that to be a claimant automatically makes a person someone who 'scrounges' off 'the taxpayer'. A rise in rhetoric about 'strivers' versus 'skivers' brings to mind the distinction between 'deserving' and 'undeserving' poor, originally enshrined in the Elizabethan Poor Law of 1601 and reinforced by the Victorian Poor Law Reform Act of 1834. A frequently used example of the undeserving, and in this sense a classic folk devil, is the stereotypical teenage single mother who gets pregnant in order to get a council flat, at the expense of hard-working families. This example persists despite there being no evidence to support it, and despite the fact that over 90% of new housing-benefit claimants in the years 2010–12 were in work (Brown, 2012). However, it works as a useful stereotype because it encapsulates several moral panics in one – teenagers having sex, non-taxpayers getting something for nothing, lazy shirkers getting more than hard-working strivers, the wrong type of women having babies, the dangers of an 'underclass' out-breeding the middle class (Arai, 2009). The stereotype also performs the two functions as outlined by Garland (2008), in that it encompasses several moral dimensions to the panic, such as people getting things they are not entitled to at the expense of those who are entitled, and it is seen as symptomatic of wider problems, in particular, problems such as inter-generational dependence on benefits and cultures of worklessness, ideas that persist despite their being shown to be inaccurate (MacDonald et al, 2013).

There is often an unspoken assumption that to be a teenage mother is to be a bad mother who lacks experience and parenting skills, and a theme in much of the research literature highlights the efforts made by young mothers to prove themselves to be 'good' mothers (Kirkman et al, 2001; Romagnoli and Wall, 2012). In addition, poor parenting has been blamed for many social ills, including the UK riots of summer 2011, with David Cameron saying about the rioters, 'Perhaps they come from one of the neighbourhoods where it's standard for children to have a mum and not a dad' (Cabinet Office, 2011a). The policy response is individualised in terms of offering parenting-skills classes, rather than addressing wider social questions, with Sarah Teather, then Children's Minister, announcing pilot parenting lessons in three areas of the country, saying that 'it is the government's moral and social duty to make sure we support all parents at this critical time' (Teather, 2011).

Evidence from research

The consequences of the moral panic around teenage pregnancy and parenting can be seen in the day-to-day lives of young people, and this chapter will now present and discuss findings from a study exploring the experience of being a young parent. Interviews and focus groups were held with young parents and parents-to-be in a city in the North of England with a reputation as a 'hot spot' for high rates of teenage pregnancy. In all, 17 people took part in interviews (nine young people and eight older family members) and two focus groups (one with five participants and one with seven) were held. The participants frequently raised issues of being judged and feeling stigmatised as a young parent by, and those issues are focused on here. Names and some other minor details have been changed to ensure anonymity.

All but one of the pregnancies of those who took part in the study had been unplanned, and participants talked about being scared to tell their parents, and also fearing what other people would say about them:

> "It was the main fact that I was scared, scared about what people are thinking and everything." (Haley, age 16, mum of Riley, age 6 months)

Several participants talked about being called offensive names at school and on social media; some had overheard comments made in the street about them being "a bit young to have a baby", or had been on the receiving end of "mucky looks" on the bus or in the street. This made them feel very conscious that they were being watched all the time and therefore had to behave in ways that would not bring further criticism upon them.

Jamie: We can't just nip to the shops, just whack any clothes on and nip to the shops –

Naomi: – if we're on our own you can do that –

Jamie: – we've got to always be at our best.

Naomi: It's like teenagers do, but when you've got the baby with you, you have to think, you always have to think what would everyone else think about what I look like today or what I'm wearing, what I'm acting like, what I'm doing, so you've always got to be conscious, you've got to care what everyone else thinks. Which isn't nice.

(Jamie, age 18, and Naomi, age 17, parents of Jordan, age 8 months)

Naomi went on to say that on first becoming a parent she had felt that everyone was looking at her and judging her and reported comments that people had made to her, with the result that she stopped leaving the house.

It was suggested that stereotypes in the popular press about young parents led to these judgements, and also led to all teenage parents being seen as the same:

"They always say 'kids having kids' and things like that. Yeah, alright, some people might not be able to cope when they are young but others can, they sort of tar you all with the same brush really and say you can't cope. I've proved a lot of people wrong." (Nikki, age 19, mum of Louise, age 3)

"There's never anything good [in the papers] – I think that's what portrays us as bad people, bad parents." (Naomi, age 17)

It is interesting to note that Naomi says that teenagers are seen as bad people as well as bad parents, which fits in with the discourse that teenagers become parents because of flaws they have, whether those be poor life-style choices or lack of ambition. Also interesting is Nikki's comment that people use the phrase 'kids having kids', a phrase that has been used by politicians in both the UK and the USA when describing teenage parents, usually disparagingly.

Jenny, age 19, the mother of Ava, age 8 weeks, described the impact of feeling judged all the time:

"When you are a young parent you feel like, personally I feel like I'm on edge all the time, thinking people are going to judge me. You hear about all these stories about young parents who get the kids taken off them and things like that, and a lot of the time people assume that you are not going to be a very good parent because you are young, so I think it makes you feel like you have to prove yourself to everyone, like when health visitors come round you have to prove that you're a good parent."

Participants were also conscious of operating within a discourse about benefit scroungers, with the stereotype being one of someone who would be claiming benefits and perhaps even deliberately getting pregnant in order to obtain access to benefits:

"When I found out I was pregnant and told one of my friends, he went 'oh, you are only doing it to get the money' and I was like 'no, I didn't do it to get the money, it wasn't meant to happen', and he was like 'people only get pregnant for money, to get a house', and all this and I was like 'well, I'm staying at home so I'm not doing it to get a house. I'm staying at home where the baby is going to be happy.'" (Zara, age 19, mum of Ellie, age 4 months)

There was strong resistance to this rhetoric, with all the young participants expressing a keen desire to go back to college or find a job, and not to be dependent on benefits:

"I do want things in life and in order to get them I need to work hard for what I want and then my family will benefit from it. I don't want to be living off the state." (Becky, age 18, pregnant)

Becky's 19-year-old partner and father of her baby was working, and they were trying to find a house together. The young fathers who were not working all reported trying to find work; several of them had had jobs but had been made redundant, or were only able to pick up short-term, insecure work. For some young people, the baby was a turning point, making them determined to get back into education when they had not previously done well, and all the young people who discussed work and education expressed a strong commitment to supporting their family.

Conclusions

The current moral panic around teenage pregnancy and parenting is closely linked to rhetoric about scroungers and the need to reduce the role of the welfare state. This rolling back of the state is partly as a result of austerity policies and partly to reduce 'cultures of dependency' and to encourage people into work. Young parents are well aware of operating within this discourse; they acknowledge the existence of stereotypes and labels attached to young parents but refuse to accept them as applying to them. However, although they resist being stereotyped, the awareness that others around them are looking at them through that lens has a profound effect on their self-perception and, in some cases (for example, Naomi), on their day-to-day lives.

These findings suggest, for social work and social policy, that there is an opportunity to support young parents to achieve their wishes. They are determined to be good parents and to demonstrate this to the outside world; they are keen to work and not be dependent on the state. However, in a context of continuing high unemployment rates for young people, with many more trapped in a cycle of low-paid, insecure work, the prospects for young parents operating in this discourse of moral panic seem bleak.

References

Arai, L. (2009) *Teenage pregnancy: The making and unmaking of a problem*, Bristol: The Policy Press.

Brown, C. (2012) 'The majority of new housing benefit claimants are in work', *Inside Housing*, www.insidehousing.co.uk/tenancies/majority-of-new-housing-benefit-claimants-in-work/6521183.article (accessed 6 January 2014).

Cabinet Office (2011a) PM's speech on the fightback after the riots, www.gov.uk/government/speeches/pms-speech-on-the-fightback-after-the-riots (accessed 25 November 2013).

Cabinet Office (2011b) David Cameron's speech on plans to improve services for troubled families, www.gov.uk/government/speeches/troubled-families-speech (accessed 4 August 2014).

Garland, D. (2008) 'On the concept of moral panic', *Crime Media Culture*, vol 4, pp 9–30.

Garthwaite, K. (2011) 'The language of shirkers and scroungers? Talking about illness, disability and Coalition welfare reform', *Disability and Society*, vol 26, no 3, pp 369–72.

Geronimus, A.T. (2003) 'Damned if you do: culture, identity, privilege, and teenage childbearing in the United States', *Social Science and Medicine*, vol 57, pp 881–93.

Goode, E. and Ben-Yehuda, N. (1994) *Moral panic: The social construction of deviance*, Oxford: Blackwell.

Ipsos-MORI (2013) *Perils of perception*, Survey for Royal Statistical Society and King's College, London.

Kirkman, M., Harrison, M., Hillier, L. and Pyett, P. (2001) '"I know I'm doing a good job": canonical and autobiographical narratives of teenage mothers', *Culture, Health and Sexuality*, vol 3, no 3, pp 279–94.

Lawlor, D.A. and Shaw, M. (2004) 'Teenage pregnancy rates: high compared with where and when?' *Journal of the Royal Society of Medicine*, vol 97, no 3, pp 121–23.

MacDonald, R., Shildrick, T. and Furlong, A. (2013) 'In search of "intergenerational cultures of worklessness": hunting the Yeti and shooting zombies', *Critical Social Policy*, vol 34, no 2, pp 199–220, doi: 10.1177/0261018313501825.

Office for National Statistics (2011) *Frequently asked questions: Births and fertility, August 2011*, London: Stationery Office.

Perrier, M. (2013) 'No right time: the significance of reproductive timing for younger and older mothers' moralities', *The Sociological Review*, vol 61, no 1, pp 69–87.

Romagnoli, A. and Wall, G. (2012) '"I know I'm a good mom": Young, low income mothers' experiences with risk perception, intensive parenting ideology and parenting education programmes', *Health, Risk and Society,* vol 14, no 3, pp 273–89.

Social Exclusion Unit (1999) *Teenage pregnancy*, London: Stationery Office.

Teather, S. (2011) 'Free parenting classes to be offered to over 50,000 mothers and fathers', https://www.gov.uk/government/news/free-parenting-classes-to-be-offered-to-over-50000-mothers-and-fathers.

Whitley, R. and Kirmayer, L.J. (2008) 'Perceived stigmatisation of young mothers: an exploratory study of psychological and social experience', *Social Science and Medicine*, vol 66, pp 339–48.

Wilson, H. and Huntington, A. (2005) 'Deviant (m)others: the construction of teenage motherhood in contemporary discourse', *Journal of Social Policy*, vol 35, no 1, pp 59–76.

FIVE

Amoral panic: the fall of the autonomous family and the rise of 'early intervention'

Stuart Waiton

Introduction

In 2008, I suggested that the concept 'moral panic' was, in many respects, past its 'sell-by' date; the idea of amoral panic was offered as an alternative (Waiton, 2008). My analysis was based on the following observations:

- the use of morality is declining as a framework for panics
- the importance of amoral categories like 'risk' and 'safety' as central tenets of panics is growing
- individuals are engaged with as diminished subjects
- old 'moral' institutions are undermined rather than shored up by these panics
- 'panics' are normalised and institutionalised.

In this chapter, I will take this argument further by examining the transformation that has been taking place in 'The Family', an institution once central to moral panic theorising, associated with moral values and understood and defended as something that was 'at the heart of society' (Goode and Ben-Yehuda, 1994, p 8). I pose the question: to what extent is the 'future of the nuclear family' the basis for panics today (Cohen, 2011, p xxii)? In particular, I look at the way the idea of the 'autonomous family' has all but disappeared from government and policy discussions of the family, and conclude by suggesting that we need to understand the rise and rise of 'early intervention' policies and initiatives as an illustration of the amoral panic that has developed around the family in the 21st century.

The rise and rise of 'early intervention'

The opening sentence of the UK government's document *Next Steps for Early Learning and Child Care*, published in 2009, reads: 'Everyone agrees that the first few months and years are the most important in a child's life.' The document goes on to explain that it is a child's mother and father that bring up a child – not governments – but then adds: 'but parents need support' (Department for Children, Schools and Families, 2009, p 3). This is just one of a plethora of documents that have been produced in recent years exploring the issue of intervention, early intervention and 'support' for families.

This mass of documents is further supported by various reports looking specifically at the issue of early intervention, one of the most noticeable being *Early Intervention: Good Parents, Great Kids, Better Citizens* (2008), written jointly by the Labour MP Graham Allen and the Conservative MP Iain Duncan Smith. This report emphasises the importance of early intervention for many of the key social policy areas in the UK. It consequently proposes a significant increase in the need to fund early-intervention initiatives. Over the period 2003–13, billions of pounds have been spent on programmes connected with early intervention, most particularly on the development of Sure Start Centres (Stewart, 2013). Strongly influenced by claims about neuroscience and the development of the infant's brain, early intervention was a central social policy in the US in the 1990s, a decade that George H.W. Bush proclaimed was to be the 'decade of the brain' (Wastell and White, 2012, p 402). In the UK, as we moved into the new millennium the then Prime Minster, Tony Blair, stated that if he had an extra billion pounds to spend, he would spend them on the under-fives (Parton, 2006, p 97).

At the level of political rhetoric (and the lack of political dissent), government policy developments, funding of social policy initiatives and, arguably, also in terms of engagement and enthusiasm among childcare professionals, early intervention has become of major significance in the UK (as it has in the US).

The autonomous family

The idea expressed in *Next Steps for Early Learning and Child Care* that 'parents need support' has become increasingly expressed in government policy documents. For example, launching Every Parent Matters in 2007, the then Education Secretary, Alan Johnson, set out the 'vital role of parents in improving their child's life chances', but also noted, 'Traditionally, parenting has been a "no-go" area for governments. But now more than ever government needs to be supportive of parents who are themselves increasingly seeking help' (Directgov, 2007). Intervention in the family and to prop up the family is not new, of course (Donzelot, 1977; Cullen, 1996). However, for much of the last two centuries there was a greater hesitancy about intervening in a unit – or, indeed, an 'institution' – that was seen as being at the 'heart of society'. For the establishment, the family was understood as a conservative body, a moral rein upon degeneracy and against militancy (Phillips, 1988). It was also seen as an important unit for developing a sense of personal responsibility and 'self-government', a liberal, Millsian 'castle' (Mill, 1999). As such, the idea of intervening in the family was (until recently) seen as problematic.

Looking at the discussion about the family in the 19th century, one gets a profound sense of how important the ideal of the autonomous ('bourgeois') family was. At a time when classical liberalism flourished, the family was seen as both an ideal and an embodiment of the bourgeois value of independence. As Berger and Berger (1983, p 110) noted, this family was protestant in nature, based on the socialisation of highly autonomous individuals; rejecting tradition, it saw action and belief as being self-generating, constructed internally by the self-piloting individual and based upon a morality of hard work, diligence, attention to detail, frugality and the systematic development of will-power. The development of strength of character was essential. The question was: how can this character be formed? The answer was simple. To have strong characters, you needed strong families. And to have strong, independent individuals, you needed the independent, private family.

The ideal of moral independence faced constant difficulties in the Victorian period with regard to the poor, with the contradictory need to support those in desperate need while maintaining personal responsibility. There was also an elitist suspicion, held by some at least, that certain sections of society lacked the capacity to develop their moral independence. However, this remained a contested area, often reflecting the elite's own belief or disbelief in the liberal project of the time (Jordon, 1974, p 25). In the main, policies demonstrated a keen interest in preserving the autonomy of families. Even where charity was given to families, this was largely done only if it could be seen to be improving rather than undermining the moral independence of those involved. In contrast to family policy developments today, it was the development of the 'character' and 'self-reliance' of parents that was seen as key, rather than the development of parenting itself (Jordon 1974, p 26).

The end of autonomy

Discussing modern-day panics in Britain and America, Joel Best argued that 'by the turn of the millennium, it was hard to identify many successful social problems campaigns mounted in either country solely by conservative claimsmakers' (Best, 2008, p x). This change can be seen with reference to the family, or what are now much more likely to be presented and discussed as 'families'. As gay marriage becomes not only legalised but promoted by the Conservative Prime Minister and Mayor of London, it is clear that traditional morality is not the force it once was. In both politics and social policy, we find little sense of an 'institution' being defended, and talk of 'The Family' has largely been replaced by the concern about 'parenting'. However, as Furedi notes, the decline of traditional morality associated with the family has not meant a decline in moralising and anxiety about families. Indeed the reverse appears to have happened, with 'virtually every social problem' becoming associated with poor parenting. Added to this, the inflated importance given to parenting (or parental determinism) as the cause and solution of social problems has resulted in 'all parents' being seen as potential problems (Furedi, 2014, p ix).

This growing problematisation and professionalisation of parenting has come, Reece (2006) argues, with what Furedi (1997) and Heartfield (2002) have described as the diminishing of subjectivity. Reece defines the modern framework for legal developments within the family as 'post-liberal'. Here she notes that not only has the conservative moral framework surrounding the family declined, but so too has the liberal sense of autonomy, privacy and responsibility that was the founding essence of the ideal 'bourgeois' family.

In her various studies of the post-liberal subject, Reece goes on to explore the ways in which the liberal subject is now conceptualised and critiqued in key political and social theories. In *Divorcing Responsibly* (2003), for example, Reece explores a variety of influential thinkers who have challenged the idea of the liberal subject, from Anthony Giddens to Catherine McKinnon, Charles Taylor and Amitai Etzioni. Rather than there being such a thing as individuals with free will, subjectivity is understood within these theories to be socially constructed, not simply in terms of individuals being merely influenced by other people and events, but to our very core and sense of self we are, these theorists argue, the product of external forces and relationships. Taken to its logical conclusion, this understanding of the subject means that the individual self or agent disappears, as does the idea that we can be responsible, as individuals, for anything. To resolve this extreme representation of the totally passive individual, Reece argues, the idea of the post-liberal subject has emerged. This post-liberal person is not a subject-less being, but nor is he or she an autonomous agent. Rather, this new subject is one that is constantly developing through continuous interactions and reflection – especially in the personal realm (Reece, 2003, pp 13–39). Rather than (conservative) morality and the liberal subject governing relationships in UK family policies, we now have the post-liberal approach, one that draws back from the idea that individuals are simply responsible for their own actions and instead understands that we are inter-subjects, subjects constantly constituted through our interactions with others, and, consequently, individuals who need to have conversations with one another. Crucially, though, these conversations are not simply between individuals but are to be encouraged, supported and facilitated by (often therapeutic) experts.

Reece illustrates the way in which the autonomous family was undermined in law from the early 1980s, when the idea of parental rights was downgraded and criticised as an 'outdated view of family life which has no part to play in a modern system of law' (Reece, 2006, p 463). Part of this downgrading of parental rights incorporated a view of a post-liberal parent – a parent who could not and should not be expected to deal with parenting matters on their own. Within this context, being a responsible parent no longer meant being autonomous, independent and self-governing, but rather the opposite. Now, the correct approach to responsible parenting was to ask for advice. 'Seeking advice', as the *Supporting Families* document explains, *is* responsible behaviour. In other words, the 'moral agent has become someone who accepts that he or she needs lessons in how to approach moral dilemmas' (Reece, 2003, p 154). Indeed a moral agent or unit (like the 'autonomous family') who believes that they do not need expert instruction has become problematic: a fiction, in the eyes of post-liberal thinkers, a delusion of grandeur that acts as a barrier to necessary support that professionals can bring.

Amoral anxiety

As the morally autonomous family declines as an ideal and as something that is expected or indeed desired, anxiety has grown about the need to support 'post-liberal' parents ever earlier in their parenting. Indeed, in Scotland new legislation has been passed giving every child a state 'named person' to oversee their interests from birth (Smith, 2014). Often framed within a 'liberal' desire to support parents, the early-intervention framework is predicated upon a diminished sense of parental capacity. Consequently, despite the focus in practice often remaining on poorer families, the trend is for the 'panic' or anxiety about parenting to be generalised – or normalised – and for state institutions to construct policy around this diminished, post-liberal subject.

Early-intervention policies and initiatives have also emerged within a context where concerns about 'risk' and 'risk focused prevention' have become influential (Farrington, 2002). Here anxieties about parents and families are expressed not through the language of morality but 'through the language of health, science and risk' (Furedi, 2011, p 96), or 'discourses of "risk" and "harm"' (Hunt, 2003, p 166). As Lee notes, unable to develop a coherent moral ideal or sense of purpose, the authorities have adopted an approach aimed at 'reducing and managing risk': the aim of moral improvement or the ideal of moral responsibility is here replaced by the ersatz value or norm of 'keeping us safe' from harm (Lee et al, 2014, p 14).

The 'scientific' basis for early intervention is provided by the use (and abuse) of neuroscience. Despite growing criticism of the illegitimate use of this science, early intervention as a core policy objective continues to grow in significance (Bruer, 1999; Wastell and White, 2012; Gillies, 2013). Where part and parcel of the Victorian moral movements, or indeed the liberal approach by individuals like John Stuart Mill, was to challenge and develop the beliefs of adults in society, today early interventionists are preoccupied merely with our behaviour; where concern used to be with the human mind, today our interventions are reduced to concerns about the biological brain (Tallis, 2012). Within this modern-day determinism, not a million miles away from the craniology of the 19th century, the understanding of humanity, of childhood, families, neighbourhoods and even society itself is reduced to an analysis of neurons.

Conclusion

The enthusiasm for early intervention can appear as a new form of dynamism in society, a new sense of purpose among professionals and a new framework for meaning and the development of grand projects.

However, predicated upon the idea that if we do not intervene in a child's life before the age of three, then it is too late, early intervention is better understood as the outcome of a collapse of belief. Biological determinism was influential in the 19th century (Lombroso, 2009), but at the same time there were competing ideas and beliefs about how to transform individuals and society. Belief in religion, or the liberal individual, or indeed in the possibility of socialism all embodied a sense of human capacity, of moral or social advancement. Similarly, with the development of the state in the 20th century there were at different times a passion for education, for social and youth work, or even for prisons, as institutions that could uplift young people and even rehabilitate adults. Today, through the prism of early intervention and the 'myth' of the first three years (Bruer, 1999), all of these forms of political, moral, individual or collective improvement are lost.

The early years framework has serious implications for the understanding of individuals and their capacity to overcome difficulties. As well as reflecting a diminished sense of the capacity for institutions, elites and beliefs to have an impact on children over the age of three, it also suggests that individuals themselves lack the capacity to change and to develop as they grow. The diminished post-liberal self is discovered in the early years interventionists who are convinced, especially with the help of brain science, that after a 'bad' first few years of life the individual is doomed to a life of antisocial behaviour (Allen and Duncan Smith, 2008).

This panic about young children and their families, expressed through a scientific and risk-based framework of early intervention, in many respects is built upon an opposition to, or at least a sense of unease about, old-fashioned traditional family values: values that can be seen as extreme, dogmatic, rigid, authoritarian and, in terms of the therapeutic idea of 'well-being' (Scottish Government, nd), potentially abusive. It likewise reacts to the ideal of autonomy and the independence of the family – a problematic place and space that takes place 'behind closed doors' and away from the ever-growing importance of professional 'support' and intervention.

I would like to end by concluding that the family today is less an institution around which moral panics can be located, than a new site for amoral elite anxieties to be expressed and the diminished subject to be kept safe.

References

Allen, G. and Duncan Smith, I. (2008) *Early intervention: Good parents, great kids, better citizens*, London: Centre for Social Justice; Smith Institute.

Berger, B. and Berger, P. (1983) *The war over the family: Capturing the middle ground*, London: Hutchison.

Best, J. (2008) 'Foreword', in S. Waiton, *The politics of antisocial behaviour: Amoral panics*, London: Routledge.

Bruer, J. (1999) *The myth of the first three years: A new understanding of early brain development and lifelong learning*, New York: The Free Press.

Cohen, S. (2011) *Folk devils and moral panics* (3rd edn) London: Routledge.

Cullen, J. (1996) 'The return of the residuum', in L. Revell and J. Heartfield (eds) *A moral impasse: The end of capitalist triumphalism*, London: Junius.

Department for Children, Schools and Families (2009) 'Summary', in *Next steps for early learning and child care*, Nottingham: DCSF Publications.

Directgov (2007) 'Department for Education and Skills recognises "Every Parent Matters"', http://webarchive.nationalarchives.gov. uk/+/www.direct.gov.uk/en/nl1/newsroom/dg_066880 (accessed 5 February 2015).

Donzelot, J. (1977) *The policing of families*, London: John Hopkins University Press.

Farrington, D.P. (2002) 'Developmental criminology and risk-focused prevention', in M. Maquire, R. Morgan and R. Reiner (eds) *The Oxford handbook of criminology* (3rd edn), Oxford: Oxford University Press.

Furedi, F. (1997) *Culture of fear: Risk-taking and the morality of low expectations*, London: Cassell.

Furedi, F. (2011) 'The objectification of fear and the grammar of morality', in S.P. Hier (ed) *Moral panics and the politics of anxiety*, London: Routledge.

Furedi, F. (2014) 'Foreword', in E. Lee, J. Bristow, C. Faircloth and J. MacVarish, *Parenting cultures*, Basingstoke: Palgrave Macmillan.

Gillies, V. (2013) 'From baby brain to conduct disorder: the new determinism in the classroom', paper presented at *Gender and Education Association Conference*, 25 April, https://www.academia.edu/3549456/From_Baby_Brain_to_Conduct_Disorder_The_New_Determinism_in_the_Classroom (accessed 3 May 2014).

Goode, E. and Ben-Yehuda, N. (1994) *Moral panic: The social construction of deviance*, Oxford: Blackwell Publishing.

Heartfield, J. (2002) *The 'death of the subject' explained*, Sheffield: Sheffield Hallam University Press.

Hunt, A. (2003) 'Risk and moralisation in everyday life', in R.V. Erikson and A. Doyle (eds) *Risk and morality*, Toronto: University of Toronto Press.

Jordon, P. (1974) *Poor parents: Social policy and the 'cycle of deprivation'*, London: Routledge.

Lee, E., Bristow, J., Faircloth, C. and MacVarish, J. (2014) *Parenting cultures*, Basingstoke: Palgrave Macmillan.

Lombroso, C. (2009) '"Criminal craniums" from Criminal Man 1876', in N. Rafter (ed) *The origins of criminology: A reader*, London: Routledge.

Mill, J.S. (1999) *On liberty*, Oxford: Oxford University Press (first published 1856).

Parton, N. (2006) *Safeguarding children: Early intervention and surveillance in a late modern society*, London: Palgrave Macmillan.

Phillips, J. (1988) *Policing the family: Social control in Thatcher's Britain*, London: Junius.

Reece, H. (2003) *Divorcing responsibly*, Oxford: Hart Publishing.

Reece, H. (2006) 'From parental responsibility to parenting responsibly', in M. Freeman (ed) *Law and sociology: Current legal issues*, Oxford: Oxford University Press, pp 459–83.

Scottish Government (nd) 'Well-being: a guide to measuring meaningful outcomes', www.scotland.gov.uk/Topics/People/ Young-People/gettingitright/background/wellbeing (accessed 24 June 2014).

Smith, E. (2014) 'Universal state guardian is a cuckoo in the nest', www.thinkscotland.org/thinkpolitics/articles.html?read_full=12373 (accessed 24 June 2014).

Stewart, K. (2013) 'Labour's record on the under fives: policy, spending and outcomes 1997–2010', LSE Social Policy Working Paper, http:// sticerd.lse.ac.uk/dps/case/spcc/wp 04.pdf (accessed 13 June 2014).

Tallis, R. (2012) *Aping mankind: Neuromania, Darwinitis and the misrepresentation of mankind*, Durham: Acumen Publishing Ltd.

Waiton, S. (2008) *The politics of antisocial behaviour: Amoral panics*, London: Routledge.

Wastell, D. and White, S. (2012) 'Blinded by neuroscience: social policy, the family and the infant brain', *Families, Relationships and Societies*, vol 1, no 3, pp 397–414.

Afterword: when panic meets practice

Maggie Mellon

I am an independent social work practitioner and commentator with a particular interest in the interface between research, policy and practice. In 2014 I was appointed as Chair of the Policy, Ethics and Human Rights Committee of the British Association of Social Workers and look forward to contributing to the promotion of ethical practice and the continuing development of professional opinion and policy. Moral panics that influence social work and social workers are clearly well within the scope of this committee and the contributions on family and gender in this byte are of great relevance to future discussion and work.

In this afterword, I have chosen to reflect particularly on the issues of widening definitions of abuse and harm, and grounds for interference and regulation of private and family life, which are raised particularly by the contributions by Tartari (Chapter One) and Waiton (Chapter Five). These chapters both describe the ways that moral panics have allowed the greater encroachment of government into private and intimate relationships. Family life has, they argue, been gripped by a succession of moral panics about everything from satanic or ritual abuse to rioting youth. Waiton goes as far as to assert that the family is 'a new site for amoral elite anxieties'. Gender relations are currently at the heart of a number of contemporary scandals, often played out as criminal trials of historical events. Tartari explores the ways in which child abuse and gender panics have the apparently paradoxical effect of over-emphasising the vulnerability of women and children and the villainy of men, to the advantage of opportunistic politicians. The contributions of Mannay (Chapter Two), Beddoe (Chapter Three) and Brown (Chapter Four) all provide additional insights into increasing government interest in, and attempts to control, family life and personal relations and the impact that this has on both individuals and families.

Suspicion of families (as 'hotbeds' of both gender and generational abuse and neglect) is now a generally accepted starting-point for social work contact with families. At a time when working and welfare poverty, malnutrition and homelessness are all increasing, so 'child protection' is now the main, if not the only, reason for social workers to be involved with families. Social work agencies seem to have prioritised protecting children from possible risk, rather than protecting families, to the extent that supporting families is not even seen as part of the role of social workers in safeguarding the welfare of children. The suspicion of fathers has become so great that depictions or descriptions of fathers in social work publications are invariably either as absent or as violent and abusive (Fatherhood Institute, 2014). Meanwhile, women have not escaped blame or the kind of stigma described by Mannay in Chapter Two; single mothers, particularly but not exclusively those on benefits, have been the object of panics and stigma under both Labour and Conservative Westminster governments. Blaming families for social problems is not, of course, a uniquely UK approach to policy, nor is blaming particular kinds of families. Beddoe's contribution in Chapter Three describes the ways in which New Zealand government policy on tackling 'problem families' demonised Maori families, thus demonstrating that 'blaming it on the family' can become blaming it on particular ethnicities, cultures or religions. Or, as Brown discusses in Chapter Four, teenage parents are held to be a bad thing not just for the young parent or their child, but also for society. But children are not only victims in a moral panic: they may also come under suspicion for the 'abuse' of other children; police in Scotland have recorded 'crimes' by children as young as three years old (*The Herald*, 2014). Waiton's family as 'a site for anxieties' thus makes the territory for social work a lot larger. Definitions of abuse and harm as grounds for social work and other official intervention in family life have stretched considerably to take in this larger ground.

Reviewing this from my own perspective of nearly 40 years' working in policy and practice in social work, it seems to me that whereas social work practice used to be concerned with working with families and individuals suffering some form of adversity, or posing risks to themselves or others, at some point in the later 20th century the family began to be understood as a risk. This does not mean that there was no oppression or injustice back then. But today, the right to private and family life seems to be increasingly seen, through official eyes at least, as a barrier to the protection of children, of women, of others described as 'vulnerable', from all sorts of risk and harm within their families and intimate relationships. Of course, no one would argue against the need for protection of children and others who cannot defend themselves from abuse. Social workers' role in this is necessary and is often done well. However, the chapters in this byte point to ways that definitions and understandings of harm, abuse and neglect, and categories of villains and victims, have been steadily widened. During one panic, *all* women and *all* children are considered vulnerable, and *all* men are suspects. During another, *all* adults are suspect of posing risk of abuse to children. In the grip of yet another panic, *all* children are made suspects in the abuse of other children. Each panic is accompanied by a new and wider definition of the problem that acts to obscure the actual risk and scale of a real problem; the perverse consequence of widening the net makes protection more rather than less difficult.

The role of children's charities as claims makers and moral entrepreneurs in this net-widening process cannot be ignored. These charities' origins in the 19th century were as rescuers of children from parental cruelty and neglect. For example, the NSPCC (National Society for the Prevention of Cruelty to Children) began its existence advocating greater prosecution of parents whose children were injured or killed because of burning or 'overlying' (that is, for being poor and not having a fireguard or a separate bed for children). Today, wider definitions and lower thresholds for intervention in relation to alleged child neglect and greater use of prosecution has become a top campaign issue for those charities. For example, the NSPCC states:

> The current legal and policy framework across the UK views neglect as a persistent behaviour with serious effects. This focus on long-term behaviour discourages early intervention, but taking action at an early stage will

significantly improve outcomes for the child. (NSPCC, 2012)

'Neglect' was defined as follows in a major report commissioned by Action for Children and the Scottish Government; this definition was subsequently used to claim a huge increase in cases of child neglect:

Neglected children include those who experience **any or all** [emphasis added] of:

- being left alone in the house or in the streets for long periods of time
- lack of parental support for school attendance
- being ignored when distressed, or even when excited or happy
- lack of proper healthcare when required
- having no opportunity to have fun with their parents or with other children. (Daniel et al, 2011)

The report goes on to warn that: 'Of all forms of maltreatment, neglect leads to some of the most profound negative and long term effects on brain and other physical development, behaviour, educational achievement and emotional well being' (Daniel et al, 2011).

Exposing a child to domestic violence is in itself now considered an act of neglect. The term 'domestic violence' is itself increasingly being used to describe non-criminal domestic arguments and skirmishes that do not involve any injury. The official definition of domestic violence was broadened in 2013 in England and Wales to include 16- and 17-year-olds and to include new forms of controlling and coercive behaviour. It states:

Any incident or pattern of incidents of controlling, coercive or threatening behaviour, violence or abuse between those aged 16 or over who are or have been intimate partners or family members regardless of gender or sexuality.

This can encompass, but is not limited to, the following types of abuse:

- psychological
- physical
- sexual
- financial
- emotional. (Home Office and Browne, 2012)

I would argue that this definition prompts a number of critical questions. For example, can anyone over 16 years old who has not been raised by wolves in the wilderness claim never to have been both a 'perpetrator' and a 'victim' of domestic violence under this definition? If every family squabble or row can be described as domestic violence, if every sexist joke or clumsy 'pass' can be described as sexual assault, if risk becomes the determinant of everything in adult–child interaction, and all adults (and children?) are held to be dangerous unless proved otherwise, I believe that serious cases can hide in plain view.

Definitions of risk and harm have also been stretched in the case of the fervour that has been created around early years policies in Scotland and England. These have been based on claims originating in the US that pre-birth and the first three years of a child's life 'hard wire' the infant's brain and largely determine her or his future. Based on this theory, intervening early in the early years to prevent harm is essential and has become a cornerstone of government policy, north and south of the border. These assertions have been debunked in a number of academic publications (for example, Wastell and White, 2012; Featherstone et al, 2012, 2013 and 2014). *Guardian* journalist Zoe Williams (2014) has also written an accessible article that summarises the arguments. In Chapter Five, Waiton points to the lack of evidence for the claims of irretrievable brain damage and lifelong harm that are now routinely directed at poor parents, that is, parents in poverty rather than bad parents. But, unfortunately, such bad science is being routinely believed and acted upon in social work decisions about children. Pre-birth or pre-discharge child protection conferences are now regularly convened on the basis of 'risks' to the child's development and attachments that 'might' exist, rather than on any actual evidence that any child has or will come to harm. These conferences consider measures (including the removal of a child at birth) that might be necessary to prevent some future *possible* harm. The victims of these decisions are usually parents in poverty and adversity, but increasingly, it seems that families who are 'different' or who oppose professionals are the target of over-zealous action. Indeed, being oppositional and hostile to professionals can now in itself be taken as evidence of risk, but so also it is claimed can 'disguised compliance', which involves appearing to agree with professionals.

Claims about the early years and the long-term irreversible damage alleged to result from neglect, alongside wider definitions of abuse, neglect and harm are now associated with the policy of earlier decisions on adoption. Rather than being used as a last resort, as the law originally intended, 'forced' adoption against the wishes of parents is being promoted as a first resort of early intervention (Narey, 2011). Social workers are tasked to ensure that plans for the adoption of children are made and carried out within 26 weeks of the child of becoming 'looked after'. This is held to be the 'child's timeframe' (Brown and Ward, 2013); the so-called evidence for a child's time frame, the now well-known image apparently showing massive differences between the brain of a neglected child and that of a normal child, is given pride of place. Nevertheless, concern for children in families with no money, no fuel, shoddy and damp housing has not gone so far as making sure that families in difficulty are offered support, and help has been given no such urgency in official or professional guidance. Benefit sanctions that leave parents without money for food, fuel, rent, fares to school are not seen as germane to child protection. 'Getting it Right for Every Child' (Scottish Government, nd), the policy in Scotland that should have heralded a move to provide support to families, has become enshrined in Scottish law as effectively a charter for professionals and not for families (Mellon, 2013a and 2013b). The term 'family' does not appear once in the Children and Young People Act 2014 that is supposed to make 'getting it right' for children a legal duty.

This brings me to my final comment and my final question. Should we not be asking why some issues that *should* have us all reaching for the panic alarm go unremarked at the time? It is only decades later that what have been real injustices and abuses come back into public view again. When this happens, we are all expected to ask 'how on earth could that have been allowed to happen'? The internment of girls in Ireland's Magdalene laundries and the forced adoption of their children, the deportation of thousands of children to the British colonies in the 20th century have all been the subject of films, documentaries, inquiries. These historic injustices all happened well into the 20th century, within living memory. So too are the now well-known abuses of children in remand homes, young offenders institutes and children's homes within the living memory of social workers. No panic alarm seemed to be sounded about these at the time, by social workers or others. The authorities of the day facilitated and funded these forced removals, separations and adoptions. The children's charities and religious orders were congratulated for their work in rescuing children and giving them 'new lives', thus ending what was held to be the 'cycle' of deprivation and depravity. Will today's fervour for early intervention and forced adoption be the scandal of tomorrow? Will social workers currently initiating or cooperating with removal at birth, with the ending of contact between parents and their children, look back and wonder why they acted in this way? Will they find themselves in front of some parliamentary inquiry, or giving evidence in a criminal trial? I would rather that we did something about it now. Tomorrow's inquiries, inquests and reviews are always too late.

References

Brown, R. and Ward, H. (2013) *Decision-making within a child's timeframe: An overview of current research evidence for family justice professionals concerning child development and the impact of maltreatment*, Working Paper 16, 2nd edn, London: Childhood Wellbeing Research Centre.

Daniel, B., Burgess, C. and Scott, J. (2011) *Review of child neglect in Scotland*, Stirling: University of Stirling.

Fatherhood Institute (2014) 'Study shows Scottish dads airbrushed out of family services' publicity', *Fatherhood Institute*, www.fatherhoodinstitute.org/2014/study-shows-scottish-dads-airbrushed-out-of-family-services-publicity.

Featherstone, B., Broadhurst, K. and Holt, K. (2012) 'Thinking systemically – thinking politically: building strong partnerships with children and families in the context of rising inequality', *British Journal of Social Work*, vol 42, no 4, pp 618–33.

Featherstone, B., Morris, K. and White, S. (2013) 'A marriage made in hell: early intervention meets child protection', *British Journal of Social Work* (advance access), doi: 10.1093/bjsw/bct052.

Featherstone, B., White, S. and Morris, K. (2014) *Re-imagining child protection: towards humane social work with families*, Bristol: Policy Press.

Home Office and Browne, J. (2012) 'New definition of domestic violence and abuse to include 16 and 17 year olds', https://www.gov.uk/government/news/new-definition-of-domestic-violence-and-abuse-to-include-16-and-17-year-olds (accessed 5 February 2015)

Mellon, M. (2013a) 'Children and young people's bill is a missed opportunity', *The Herald* (24 May), www.heraldscotland.com/comment/columnists/children-and-young-people-bill-is-a-missed-opportunity.21163028.

Mellon, M. (2013b) 'Serviceland. The dark world of the named person', *Scottish Review* (18 December), www.scottishreview.net/MaggieMellon137.shtml.

Narey, M. (2011) 'The Narey Report. A blueprint for the nation's lost children', *The Times* (5 July), www.thetimes.co.uk/tto/life/families/article3083832.ece (or access the report at: www.mnarey.co.uk/adoption-advisor.php).

NSPCC (National Society for the Prevention of Cruelty to Children) (2012) *CORE-INFO: Emotional neglect and emotional abuse in pre-school children*, London: NSPCC.

Scottish Government (nd) 'Getting it right for every child', www.scotland.gov.uk/Topics/People/Young-People/gettingitright/background (accessed 5 February 2015).

The Herald (2014) 'The terrible three-year-olds: police record five toddlers committing offences' (29 May), www.heraldscotland.com/news/home-news/the-terrible-three-year-olds-police-record-five-toddlers-committing-offences.1401357096.

Wastell, D. and White, S. (2012) 'Blinded by neuroscience: social policy, the family and the infant brain', *Families, Relationships and Societies*, vol 1, no 3, pp 397–414.

Williams, Z. (2014) 'Is misused neuroscience defining early years and child protection policy?' *The Guardian* (26 April), www.theguardian.com/education/2014/apr/26/misused-neuroscience-defining-child-protection-policy.